Hallelujah!
Amen.
It is Done.

Daily Enjoying His Presence

Let us pray and enjoy His presence.
Love & Prayers,
Judy

JUDITH ELMER

D1367768

ISBN: 1449985297
ISBN-13: 9781449985295
Library of Congress Control Number: 2009914007

Dedication

This book is written to bring honor and glory to Jesus Christ.

Contents

All scriptures are taken from The New International Version of the Bible. (NIV)

Introduction

Do you believe in the power of prayer? I bet you do, or you wouldn't be holding this book. I believe in the power of prayer, too. This book is a call, inviting believers to come together in prayer. We can expect powerful effects when believers come together to:

praise Him...*Hallelujah!*
surrender to His will...*Amen.*
and live in faith as His plan unfolds...*It is Done.*

God is able to do anything and everything on His own, yet He chooses to work through the prayers of His people. What a Gracious God! Prayer is a powerful spiritual weapon designed by God to:

strengthen our faith,
unite us in faith,
and encourage us as we live by faith.

Hallelujah! Amen. It is Done. is an invitation to daily enjoy God's presence, practice listening to Him, and to lock our hearts together in prayer. When God's children pray in agreement with His Word...that's powerful prayer! Let us position ourselves to sense His presence and hear Him speak to our hearts. There is great joy cheering the Holy Spirit on!

LET US PRAY!

WHEN WE PRAY...
WE ARE AN ANSWER TO JESUS' PRAYER

Many years ago the Holy Spirit whispered into my heart that He was going to teach me about joy and prayer. At the time I didn't know that the two were so closely related. I'm excited about what the Holy Spirit has taught me and is continuing to teach me about joy and prayer. One thing you need to know: I'm a work in progress. I'm a follower of Jesus, learning and growing. The Holy Spirit in His infinite grace allows me, as well as you, to pray with Him, and being with Him can bring a deep sense of joy. I'd like to share with you the joy I've experienced by being with Jesus the One True God.

God wants us to be with Him, more than anything else. He wants us to have a personal relationship with Him through Jesus Christ. Every time I think of that, I'm amazed and reminded of His Great Love and Grace.

Creator God,

King of Kings,

the Messiah wants to be with me, and you!

This is demonstrated in the book of John when Jesus prayed, **"Father, I want those you have given me to be with me where I am"** (John 17:24). I'm sure glad He prayed that prayer for me. He prayed that prayer for you, too. That great intercessory prayer of Jesus' is an awesome example of His everlasting love and His deep desire to be with us.

Jesus also prayed, **"That all of them may be one, Father, just as you are in me and I am in you. May they also be in us so that the world may believe that you have sent me. I have given them the glory that you gave me, that**

Hallelujah! Amen. It is Done.

they may be one as we are one: I in them and you in me. May they be brought to complete unity to let the world know that you sent me and have loved them even as you have loved me" (John 17:21-23). What a Gracious God! Jesus' prayer was a cry for us to be...united in love with Him, united in love with fellow believers, and for our lives to be a powerful witness of God's great love in action.

Intercessory prayer is love in action! When those in Christ pray in agreement with the will of our Father, they stand one with Him and stand united in faith with each other. That's powerful prayer! When we pray, it's as if the Father says with excitement:

"Listen to My precious children!"

"They are with Me!"

"They agree with Me."

"They're ready."

"It's time."

WHEN WE PRAY...WE ARE AN ANSWER TO JESUS' PRAYER!

Hallelujah!

"Hallelujah! For our Lord God Almighty reigns." (Rev. 19:6)

Praise is a spiritual weapon that clears the way for the Holy Spirit to do His work. When we praise Him, we're like John the Baptist calling out, **"Prepare the way for the Lord, make straight paths for him"** (Mark 1:3). God gives us the "wonder-full" privilege of joining Him in His kingdom work.

He is Lord God.

He is King.

He is Almighty.

Yet, He still grants us the privilege of coming alongside of Him as He works. We praise Him for being a relational God!

The power of praise is evident throughout the Bible. One example is when Paul and Silas were in prison, and they decided to pray and praise God. **"About midnight Paul and Silas were praying and singing hymns to God, and the other prisoners were listening to them. Suddenly there was such a violent earthquake that the foundations of the prison were shaken. At once all the prison doors flew open, and everybody's chains came loose"** (Acts 16:25-26). God chose to release His power. Praise pushes back the schemes of the devil and ushers in the work of God.

The Psalms are full of praise. We learn in the Psalms that God willingly releases His power when we honestly and humbly come before Him in praise. When we praise God we focus on Him, and not ourselves. Things change when we focus on God and His attributes. Taking our eyes off our circumstances and looking to God puts things in the right perspective. The truth about who God is enables us to rest in His joy, regardless of our circumstances. His Love doesn't change. He is the Joy-Giver. He's the One who gives a deep sense of well-being, and whispers within our soul…"My child, everything's going to be okay."

Did you know that Jesus sang? He and His disciples sang after the Passover meal. Don't you wish you could have heard that singing? I had never thought about Jesus singing, until I read *"When they had sung a hymn, they went out to the Mount of Olives"* (Matt. 26:30). Jesus and His disciples ended their last supper together in praise. Isn't it worth pondering the importance of praise if Jesus Himself sung praises to the Father?

When believers unite in praise, expect great things! God's Word says in Psalm 8 and 22 that God has ordained praise and He inhabits the praises of His people. In addition, we don't want to overlook the great exhortation found in Luke 19 that says if we don't praise Him, the rocks will cry out in praise!

Therefore, as God's redeemed, we are motivated and privileged to praise Him. Let us join the great multitude we read about in Revelation 19. Let our prayers be: *"like the roar of rushing waters, and like loud peals of thunder, shouting:"*

"Hallelujah! For our Lord God Almighty reigns." (Rev. 19:6)

Amen.

For no matter how many promises God has made, they are "Yes" in Christ. And so through him the "Amen" is spoken by us to the glory of God. (2 Cor. 1:20)

I have said "Amen" so many times without really knowing the impact of that word. When we say "Amen," we're really saying, "So be it." Wow! Letting go of our control and surrendering to God's way is an important component of prayer. There is power in submission. The Holy Spirit enables us to humbly say, "Amen" or "So be it." A perfect example of this kind of prayer comes from Jesus Himself in the Garden of Gethsemane. **"Going a little farther, he fell with his face to the ground and prayed, "My Father, if it is possible, may this cup be taken from me. Yet not as I will, but as you will"** (Matt. 26:39). Jesus knew the intense agony that was ahead of Him. His words **"not as I will, but as you will"** and His obedience expressed a resounding "Amen" in the ears of Father God.

Jesus was broken for us. He chose to completely surrender to the will of the Father. That's brokenness. The Bible teaches that "broken people" are blessed! **"Blessed are the poor in spirit, for theirs is the kingdom of heaven"** (Matt.5:3). People "poor in spirit" are humbly broken. This is a good thing. The opposite of brokenness is self-centeredness or pride. In order that nothing hinders our prayers, it is important that we humble ourselves before God. Broken people come honestly before Him, with no excuses, agreeing with Him about the areas of their lives that need to be more like Him. **"The sacrifices of God are a broken spirit; a broken and contrite heart, O God, you will not despise"** (Psalm 51:17). God is looking for broken prayer warriors.

The scripture says *"the 'Amen' is spoken by us,"* pointing to the importance and power of believers praying together. Prayer is a spiritual union with Jesus Christ and fellow believers. Praying together doesn't necessarily mean that we have to be in the same room. We can pray and still be together even if we're physically far apart. Prayer is not limited by distance. We can join fellow believers anywhere in the world and pray, because the Holy Spirit of Jesus lives within the hearts of believers. I'm excited about you and me coming together in prayer. One purpose for writing this book of daily intercessory prayers is for us to come together, united in faith and pray in agreement. There is power in prayer when His children humbly agree with His will.

Many prayers in the Bible are graciously sprinkled with "together" words: our, we, us, and they. For example:

Our Father in heaven, hallowed be your name. (Matt. 6:9)

We always thank God, the Father of our Lord Jesus Christ, when we pray for you.

(Col. 1:3)

Forgive us our debts, as we also have forgiven our debtors. And lead us not into temptation, but deliver us from the evil one. (Matt. 6:12-13)

Before they call I will answer; while they are still speaking I will hear. (Isaiah 65:24)

And so through him the "Amen" is spoken by us to the glory of God. (2 Cor. 1:20)

It is Done.

"So is my word that goes out from my mouth: It will not return to me empty, but will accomplish what I desire and achieve the purpose for which I sent it." (Isaiah 55:11)

One way I like to express the meaning of "it is done," is to say "in His time," or "God does what He says." In other words...

God is in control.

He doesn't change.

And, *"the word of the Lord stands forever"* (1 Peter 1:25).

In 1996, I started to keep a journal, and I continue to do so. My original intention for writing was to become more aware of God's presence in my life, along with His blessings. I came to realize that the evil one loves to twist things around and steal our joy. Oftentimes his battlefield is our mind, and his primary weapon is doubt. He uses any tactic he can to discourage us from knowing the truth. This is evident in the Garden of Eden when he said to Eve, *"Did God really say, 'You must not eat from any tree in the garden'?"* (Gen. 3:1). Journal writing became a spiritual warfare weapon for me. I discovered that writing down the evidence of God's presence in my life and the scriptures that He whispered into my mind was a powerful defense against doubt. Having those special scriptures written down and then rereading God's words served as a safeguard against the enemy stealing my joy. The Holy Spirit used journal writing as a tool that enabled me to say with confidence and joy:

God's Word is true.

He cannot lie.

It is done!

As the years passed, my journal writing took a new direction. I started to write prayers. The Holy Spirit, my

Teacher, began to show me "snapshots," picturing a certain encouragement, need, or circumstance for which to pray. After I received an assignment to pray, He impressed on my heart to write the prayer down. Over the years, my Teacher guided my thoughts and heart as He designed these prayers written in this book. God really does what He says He will do. Long ago He told me He was going to teach me about joy and prayer. I am His student...learning and growing.

An important truth I've learned is that whatever is seen in the supernatural or whatever is impressed in minds and hearts must line up and fall within the boundaries of the written Word of God. If it doesn't, then dismiss it...throw it out! The Bible is God's voice and His will for us. God does speak. And there is no greater joy than to recognize His voice!

His Word...
produces change,
makes satan run,
saves,
delivers,
encourages,
guides,
comforts,
and even more!

God's Word has the power to shape and mold you into that beautiful free person He created you to be. Jesus taught us a lot about the power of God's Word when He was tempted by satan in the desert. Jesus spoke sacred scriptures and defeated the temptations of the devil. The Word of God is true, and the evil one can't stand to be around the truth. However, to use God's Word effectively, you must have faith in Jesus and all that He has done. You must believe what you're saying. Anyone can quote a scripture verse. Faith in Jesus as your personal Lord and

Savior and knowing and obeying God's Word is what makes scriptures a powerful weapon.

God is delighted when we pray back His Word. For those who have children, grandchildren, nieces, or nephews, do you remember how you felt when they first said your name? I repeated the words over and over to my boys: "Ma-Ma," "Ma-Ma." Then when the day finally came and they said "Ma-Ma," my heart melted. If that's the way we feel when our children or other family members say back the words we want them to say, can you imagine the power released when we pray back God's words! Echoing back the words of God with a childlike faith is a powerful prayer. You can rest knowing that He hears your prayers because you're trusting in what He says. ***"This is the confidence we have in approaching God: that if we ask anything according to his will, he hears us"*** (1 John 5:14).

God's Word generates joy...that deep sense that everything's going to be okay even when feelings and circumstances say something different. We can rest in the joy that comes from knowing the truth of His Word.

The truth is...
<u>We have eternal life through Jesus Christ</u>.
Jesus said to her, "I am the resurrection and the life. He who believes in me will live, even though he dies; and whoever lives and believes in me will never die." (John 11:25-26)

The truth is...
<u>God forgives</u>.
If we confess our sins, he is faithful and just and will forgive us our sins and purify us from all unrighteousness. (1 John 1:9)

The truth is…
God can take intended harm and turn it to good.
And we know that in all things God works for the good of those who love him, who have been called according to his purpose. (Rom. 8:28)

The truth is…
He will always be with us.
"Never will I leave you; never will I forsake you." (Heb. 13:5)

The truth is…
God restores us.
The LORD is my shepherd, I shall not be in want. He makes me lie down in green pastures, he leads me beside quiet waters, he restores my soul. (Psalm 23:1-3)

God cannot lie.
He said His Word will not return to Him empty.
God's Word will accomplish what He desires and achieve His purpose.
We believe.
Therefore, in joy we can say
"It is done!"

The Joy of Listening

"I am the good shepherd. The good shepherd lays down his life for the sheep.
My sheep listen to my voice; I know them, and they follow me." (John 10:11, 27)

Years ago when I heard someone say they heard God speak, it made me feel nervous. I thought, Oh my, they're hearing voices! But as I studied God's Word, I learned that God is a speaking God. It's natural for God to speak. In the book of Genesis, God spoke things into existence. For example: **"And God said, 'Let there be light,' and there was light"** (Gen. 1:3). In the book of Exodus, God and Moses had conversations with each other, like friends do.

Oftentimes, God speaks to us by placing thoughts in our minds and impressions on our hearts. These thoughts or impressions can be so strong in our "spiritual ears" that it's like hearing Him speak. When this happens, we say we heard His voice. Keep in mind that our hearts can deceive us and our minds can get confused. Therefore, we must test what we hear according to the truth of God's written Word. If what we are hearing with our "spiritual ears" does not line up and fall within the boundaries of God's written Word, then dismiss it…throw it out!

God is able to speak to us any way He chooses. His voice is heard…

in the words of scripture,
through prayer,
through life's circumstances,
through godly people,
in songs of worship,
in dreams and visions,
and through the Church.

God values communication. Healthy relationships involve both speaking and listening. Jesus taught the importance of listening by describing Himself as the Good Shepherd and believers as His sheep. Jesus said, **"My sheep listen to my voice; I know them, and they follow me"** (John 10:27). What a tender illustration of God's deep desire for us to have a healthy relationship with Him. God wants us to enjoy both speaking to Him and listening to Him. He wants us to enjoy being with Him. When we place our faith in Jesus, as our Savior and Lord, we can be confident that we are one of His sheep. Therefore, we have the assurance that we can hear Him as He speaks to us personally throughout the pages of the Bible. The Good Shepherd loves us. He brings joy and comfort to our souls as we follow Him. No matter how big our problems, they're not too big for the shoulders of our Good Shepherd who...

listens to us,

speaks to us,

guides us,

corrects us,

cares for us,

protects us,

and willingly laid down His life for us.

Even when life's painful circumstances remain the same, we can count on God keeping His Word. Therefore, we can choose to live a life of joy. Our source of joy is Jesus. He gives that deep sense of well-being. He is the Joy-Giver.

Listening to God brings great joy!

My Testimony...Like Clay

Have you ever watched a potter take a lump of clay and mold and shape it into something beautiful and useful? My husband is a gifted potter. I've learned from watching him at the wheel that change for the clay begins when the potter touches the clay.

I grew up feeling worried, guilty and scared. I thought that if something wasn't right in my life, I needed to fix it. The message I received as a young girl growing up was "be perfect, you're responsible." Yet, the harder I tried to be perfect and get things right, the more I worried and messed things up. I thought God was asking for <u>me</u> to get myself together, for <u>me</u> to do the fixing, for <u>me</u> to do the changing. I was trying, but it wasn't working. I was listening to a lie and didn't even know it. I didn't know the truth of God's Word. I felt like a powerless lump of clay.

In a moment of surrender, I climbed up on the Master Potter's wheel. Just like that clay, I chose to yield to the Potter's Hands and allow Him to open me up to the truth of His Word. I began my search for the truth. I knew I needed to know the truth about God before I could recognize a lie. I wanted to be free from worry, guilt, and fear. I wanted to know the truth about Jesus and His grace and power.

Just like a potter, the Holy Spirit began to pull me up and out of lies. Piece by piece, He replaced lies with the truth. The first truth that God spoke into my heart was, *"The thief comes only to steal and kill and destroy; I have come that they may have life, and have it to the full"* (John 10:10). God, the Master Potter, used this truth to begin the process of pulling me up and out of worry, guilt and fear. As I prayed and studied His Word, I could sense His Hands molding and shaping my life with His joy.

The truth is...Jesus is the Joy-Giver. His Word is true. "**Then you will know the truth, and the truth will set you free**" (John 8:32).   I experienced freedom when I discovered that Jesus wanted me to come to Him with all my failures and imperfections. He's the One who is perfect, not me. Jesus does the fixing. It's His Holy Spirit that enables me to change.

I've also come to realize that change takes time and can be painful. It takes time for the potter to work the lumps out of the clay while reshaping the clay into a beautiful, useful vessel. Furthermore, if the clay is not centered on the wheel, it fights the hands of the potter. I'm so grateful that our Master Potter has given us four major ways to stay centered on Him: Bible study, prayer, Christian fellowship, and praise. Over the years I've learned that staying centered on Jesus is how I can have life to the fullest. I'm not talking about a life filled with material things, because real joy is not found in material things. I'm not talking about a life completely free from pain and struggles, because we're still in this world. Instead, I'm talking about resting in the truth of God's Word. I can live in joy because He says...

I love you.
I am with you.
I will pull you through.

Jesus said, "**I have come that they may have life, and have it to the full**" (John 10:10). I can see how God has manifested the truth of this scripture in my life.

First of all I have life...eternal life.
I have eternal life not because I've earned it, or because of any good deeds.
I have eternal life because I agree with God about my sins.
I choose to turn away from those sins.
I have eternal life because I've placed my faith in Jesus.
He died for my sins and rose from the dead.

He's alive now.
I accept His grace.
He is my Savior.
I don't understand all His ways, yet I choose to trust Him.
He is my Lord.
I will follow Him.

The next part of that scripture reads, "...*and have it* [life] *to the full."* As the years pass, I continue to sense His Hands shaping and molding my life with His truth. I have come to realize that life to the full is lived in His spiritual blessings:

the joy of His presence,
the depth of His love,
the power of His forgiveness,
the strength of His peace,
the blessings of His guidance,
and even more!

Jesus came so we could have life to the full...a life lived in His spiritual blessings. He is the Giver of fullness of life. God's Word says to all who by grace through faith receive Jesus as their Savior and Lord...

You have eternal life. (John 3)
I have prepared a place for you. (John 14)
I will never leave you. (Heb. 13)
I am with you always. (Matt. 28)

Following Jesus and becoming more like Him is a lifelong process. I'm not finished. I'm on the Master Potter's wheel. Some days are better than others. How easy it is to focus on people and circumstances instead of looking to Jesus. Allowing God to trim away those areas in my life that need to be more like Him can be painful. Yet, what I've found to be true is that God is our Greatest Encourager. Once again the truth of His Word brings great comfort. *"Being confident of this, that he who began a good work in you will carry it on to completion until the day of Christ Jesus"* (Phil. 1:6). This truth rises up in my soul when thoughts or feelings want to take me back to old lies. My prayer is that the truth of His Word will rise up in your soul, too, and you will live a life in joy. Let us listen to our Master Potter as He lovingly whispers into our souls...

"It's okay."

"I'm not finished with you."

"My grace is sufficient."

Before We Begin

Once again, I'm excited about praying together and seeking God's voice.

Before we begin, I would like to share my threefold purpose for writing this book, as well as my desire and my prayer for you, the reader.

1. This book is an invitation to pray together.
When we agree in faith, and agree with His will, we can expect His power to be released.
The prayer of a righteous man is powerful and effective. (James 5:16)

2. This book is an invitation to daily enjoy His presence.
God promises that He is with us. Awareness of His presence brings great joy and peace.
The Lord is near. (Phil. 4:5)

3. This book is an invitation to practice listening to God.
Come before the Lord in humble agreement about the areas of your life that need to be more like Him. You are encouraged to still yourself before the Lord, expecting Him to speak.
He wakens me morning by morning, wakens my ear to listen like one being taught. (Isaiah 50:4)

[As a reminder: whatever is impressed in your mind or heart must line up and fall within the boundaries of the written Word of God. If it doesn't, then dismiss it...throw it out! The Word of God is truth. The Bible is God's voice and His will for us.]

You will notice that after each prayer there's a special space provided for you to write down what God impressed in your mind or heart. I want to encourage you to start out by writing down one word that came to your mind after reading the scripture, or the prayer, or the title. As you continue to daily meet with God, after reading the prayer for that day, I encourage you to write one or two lines of praise and thanksgiving in the space provided. Or, in the space provided you can even express your fears and pain. You may find yourself writing prayers, as the Holy Spirit leads you. My hope is that you will look forward to this time. This is not a task. Instead, this time of listening and journaling is about relationship between you and the Holy Spirit. There is no greater joy than to sense His presence and hear God speak.

My desire for you is...

to encounter God's infinite grace,
to daily enjoy His presence,
for prayer to be an inspiring daily habit,
to practice the joy of listening,
and to be strengthened in faith.

My prayer for you is...

Gracious Father, I praise You for Your Everlasting Love.
You want to be with us.
You are near.
You walk beside us.
You go in front of us and behind us.
Your presence surrounds us.
Even when we don't feel Your closeness, You are still
near.
Create in us a desire to spend time with You.
Help us to pray each day.
Teach us to listen to You.
Thank You for speaking to us through the pages of the
Bible.
Fill us daily with joy that only You can give.
Breathe on us.
Sing over us.
Bless us with an awareness of Your presence.
Thank You, Jesus, for the peace and joy found near Your
heart.

**"Ask and you will receive, and your joy will be
complete."** (John 16:24)

Hallelujah! Amen. It is Done.

Daily Prayers

January

Photo by Linda Estes

Praise Him...*Hallelujah!*
Surrender to His will...*Amen.*
Live in faith as His plan unfolds...*It is done.*

January 1

Forbid

Father, You are God.
You are the Commander.
You have Authority over all people and all creation.
Your Power is unlimited.
When we repent of our sins, and in faith accept Jesus as our Savior and Lord,
Your Power lives within us.
Because of Your great Love, You give us Your Power to overcome.
Lord Jesus, we join You in prayer as You forbid the schemes of the evil one to destroy us.
We join You as You constantly intercede for us.
Hold back and tie up the enemy for us.
We join You as You release Your Peace and Joy.
Help us to remember always that this all-surpassing Power comes from You!

But we have this treasure in jars of clay to show that this all-surpassing power is from God and not from us. (2 Cor. 4:7)

Enjoy His presence: still yourself, listen, write

Hallelujah! Amen. It is Done.

January 2

Freedom

We praise You Father for Your All-Surrounding perfect presence.
You've got us covered and completely guarded.
Your Hand cannot be removed because Your Power is greater
than any other power in the world!
We praise You for reaching down and pulling us up and out of
the pit of...
lies,
depression,
loneliness,
abuse,
and unforgiveness.
Jesus, You are the Only One who sets people free.
Praise You for giving us joy and peace in the middle of pain and
suffering.
Praise You for the power and strength that is ours through Jesus
Christ.

*He lifted me out of the slimy pit, out of the mud and mire;
he set my feet on a rock and gave me a firm place to
stand. He put a new song in my mouth, a hymn of praise
to our God.* (Psalm 40:2-3)

Enjoy His presence: still yourself, listen, write

January 3

Faithfulness

Faithful Father, You stick with us all the time.
You never turn away from us.
Your Faithfulness is beyond our capabilities.
Even when we're not faithful, You are still faithful.
Jesus' Blood covers us with Grace and Mercy.
Help us to follow Your lead.
We want to walk in the direction You planned for us even before we were born.
Help our families remain faithful to You.
We want what You want in our lives.
We choose to trust You.
Your Love and Faithfulness is forever and ever.

For the LORD is good and his love endures forever; his faithfulness continues through all generations. (Psalm 100:5)

Enjoy His presence: still yourself, listen, write

Hallelujah! Amen. It is Done.

January 4

Still the Same

Father we praise You for never changing.
Your Love is constant.
You don't love us one day, and not love us the next day.
Remind us that Your Love and Power is the same...
today,
yesterday,
and tomorrow.
Remind us of how You pulled us up and out of awful situations.
Bring to our minds the times in our lives when Your Love and Power was so evident.
Help us Lord to always remember what You've done for us.
Rekindle in us a spirit of hope and newness.
Help us to look ahead in joy and peace, for the best is yet to come.

Jesus Christ is the same yesterday and today and forever.
(Heb. 13:8)

Enjoy His presence: still yourself, listen, write

Covered

Jesus we praise You for being so Gracious to us.
Thank You for picking us up and dusting us off.
Thank You for Your Power and Strength.
Thank You for covering us with Your Love...forever.
Lord Jesus...
take away,
brush off,
block out,
anything that would steal our peace and joy.
Press in our minds that we are safe with You.
We are covered by Your Mighty Hand.
You are Faithful.

He will cover you with his feathers, and under his wings you will find refuge; his faithfulness will be your shield and rampart. (Psalm 91:4)

Enjoy His presence: still yourself, listen, write

Hallelujah! Amen. It is Done.

January 6

Be Still

Father, You are the Mighty Warrior.
You are fighting for people at all times.
Thank You, Holy Spirit, for constantly praying for us.
We can rest in knowing that the battle is Yours and not ours.
You are the Vine, and like branches, we are securely connected to You.
Help us to receive all that You desire for us.
We want to be filled with Your characteristics.
We want to have peace of mind and have a supernatural love for people.
Give us patience when we don't feel like waiting.
Enable us to lead a well-balanced life for You.
Create in us a desire to seek Your approval only and not worry about what others think.
You are God Most High.
Still our minds and bring rest to our hearts.
You are God.

"Be still, and know that I am God." (Psalm 46:10)

Enjoy His presence: still yourself, listen, write

January 7

Breakthrough

We praise You Jesus, our Living Word, our Rock.
You came to testify to the truth.
You are Truth.
You are All-Powerful.
You satisfy and sustain us.
You pray for us day and night.
You are seated at the right Hand of God.
You are the Hammer that breaks through any hard walls of...
anger,
bitterness,
or confusion.
Thank You for this holy privilege of joining You in prayer.
Use these prayers to break through walls in the minds and hearts of people.
May they respond to Your Living Water that quenches the thirstiest mind and the driest heart.
Jesus is the Living Water that...
cleanses us from sin,
delivers us from evil,
and empowers us to live a life of joy and peace.
We praise You Jesus, our Breakthrough God.

"Is not my word like fire," declares the LORD, "and like a hammer that breaks a rock in pieces?" (Jer. 23:29)

Enjoy His presence: still yourself, listen, write

Hallelujah! Amen. It is Done.

January 8

When I Feel Empty

Father, You know that at times our Christian walk can be hard.
Sometimes we feel empty and tired.
Some things we don't understand.
But the truth is that You Love us, and Your thoughts and ways are higher than ours.
Your Word tells us that the Christian life is not a sprint.
Instead, the Christian life is like a long-distance run.
And You give us everything we need through Jesus Christ.
Through Him we have the Power to overcome sin and grow stronger in Him.
Thank You for Your Word that fills our empty hearts with the truth that...
encourages,
guides,
and strengthens.
We trust You Jesus.
Open our minds and fill our empty souls.

I am the LORD your God, who brought you up out of Egypt. Open wide your mouth and I will fill it. (Psalm 81:10)

Enjoy His presence: still yourself, listen, write

January 9

The Kiss

Father God, You are Love.
You created us to love one another.
Father, help married couples stay in love.
Protect couples from hurts that cause a wedge between them.
May they enjoy tender moments together.
We praise You Father, for making expressions of love so enjoyable.
Your Love brings joy to marriages.
Your Love brings peace and contentment.
Your Love teaches us how to love.

Let him kiss me with the kisses of his mouth--- for your love is more delightful than wine. (Song of Songs 1:2)

Enjoy His presence: still yourself, listen, write

Hallelujah! Amen. It is Done.

January 10

Consecrate Your Heart

Father we worship You.
You are God, our One and Only King.
You have always been.
You are now and forever.
You are the Only One worthy of our worship.
You are Most High.
We adore You.
We bow down to You and ask You to purify our hearts.
We want to consecrate our hearts to You.
We dedicate the core of our being to You.
We desire to love You with all our hearts.
Help us to love one another with a deep sacrificial love.
O God, keep our hearts from hardening and becoming cold.
Enable us to forgive others and ourselves.
Cleanse us from within.
Change our hearts.
Make us more like Jesus.

Create in me a pure heart, O God, and renew a steadfast spirit within me. (Psalm 51:10)

Enjoy His presence: still yourself, listen, write

Guilt Remover

Merciful Father, words cannot fully express Your Love for us.
You treat us in ways we don't deserve.
You are Gracious.
You loved us so much that You gave us Jesus.
He is the Lamb of God...the Perfect Sacrifice for our sins.
Jesus not only forgives our sin, He takes away the guilt of our sin too.
He forgives and forgets.
Help us to forgive ourselves.
You can desensitize our feelings of guilt.
You want us to agree with you about our sins and turn from them.
After we've confessed our sin to You, release us from beating ourselves for that sin, over and over, again and again.
You brush away our guilt.
Jesus is the Guilt Remover.
May we accept and receive Your Gift of Grace.

I said, "I will confess my transgressions to the LORD"--- and you forgave the guilt of my sin. (Psalm 32:5)

Enjoy His presence: still yourself, listen, write

Hallelujah! Amen. It is Done.

January 12

Ground Servants

Father, thank You for giving us Jesus.
He is our Solid Rock.
He is our Firm Foundation.
Strengthen our faith and ground us in the truth of Your Word.
Help us to be more like Jesus.
Enable us to die to ourselves and become Christ-like servants.
May we be willing to let You grind away in us anything that is not pleasing to You.
Change us, Lord, and fill us up with Your Spirit, so we can better serve Your sheep.
We choose to be Christ-centered servants, who humbly feed Your sheep with the truth of Your Word.

The third time he said to him, "Simon son of John, do you love me?" Peter was hurt because Jesus asked him the third time, "Do you love me?" He said, "Lord, you know all things; you know that I love you." Jesus said, "Feed my sheep." (John 21:17)

Enjoy His presence: still yourself, listen, write

Marching for Jesus

Father, we worship You, and You alone.
Worthy is the Lamb!
You are the One and Only.
You are Most High.
You are the Ancient of Days.
We praise You for gathering the youth of today.
You are preparing them and making them ready for the days to come.
Holy Spirit, You are bringing them to the truth.
By Your Power, may we move forward together for Your Namesake.
We want You to lead because the battle is Yours.
May Your presence guide us, as we choose to march for Jesus.

All the earth bows down to you; they sing praise to you, they sing praise to your name. Come and see what God has done, how awesome his works in man's behalf! (Psalm 66:4-5)

Enjoy His presence: still yourself, listen, write

Hallelujah! Amen. It is Done.

January 14

Gathering

Father, You want us to be with You.
You created us to be together...together with You and together with other believers.
Repenting of our sins, and placing our faith and trust in Jesus, makes us part of Your family.
We ask that people...
turn from their sins,
in faith accept Jesus as their personal Savior,
make Him Lord of their lives,
and follow Him.
We praise You, Holy Spirit, for Your perfect timing and Powerful ways of gathering Your children.

He who is not with me is against me, and he who does not gather with me scatters. (Matt. 12:30)

Enjoy His presence: still yourself, listen, write

January 15

Measure of Faith

Father, thank You and praise You for Jesus, our Indescribable Gift!
Thank You, Jesus, for loving us so much that You died for our sins.
Thank You, Father, for looking at us through eyes of grace.
We are eternally grateful for Your great Love for us.
Help Your children to respect one another and stick together.
We desire to be united in You.
We want Your Power to be reflected through us...the Body of Christ.
Each one of us is needed and valuable to You.
Teach us to use Your Power to glorify You, and serve others.
With our measure of faith, may we always look to You.

For by the grace given me I say to every one of you: Do not think of yourself more highly than you ought, but rather think of yourself with sober judgment, in accordance with the measure of faith God has given you. (Romans 12:3)

Enjoy His presence: still yourself, listen, write

Hallelujah! Amen. It is Done.

January 16

Authority

All Authority has been given to You, O God.
You are Above All.
You are the King.
You are in the position of Authority, seated at the right hand.
You are the Great I AM.
Your dominion is Powerful and Everlasting.
Your kingdom will never be destroyed.
You will reign forever.
Help our nation to recognize the lies of the enemy.
No man will be or ever has been above You.
O God, help us to focus on Jesus, our First Love.
Remind us that this nation is under God's Authority.

The earth is the LORD'S, and everything in it, the world, and all who live in it. (Psalm 24:1)

Enjoy His presence: still yourself, listen, write

Christian Order

Thank You, Father, that our steps are secure with Jesus.
Our faith in Him brings true security.
Our schedule and timing is secure with Him.
You have good plans for us.
Every one of our days have been ordained by You.
You have our best interests in mind.
Your order in the universe, family, and government is perfect.
Help us not to worry about time.
Free us, O God, from being so busy.
Help us make our time with Jesus our top priority.
He is the Rock that brings order in our lives and gives us that steady place to stand.

He set my feet on a rock and gave me a firm place to stand. (Psalm 40:2)

Enjoy His presence: still yourself, listen, write

Hallelujah! Amen. It is Done.

His House

Father, You are the Builder of everything.
You're our Solid Foundation.
Jesus is the Cornerstone.
We want to be like living stones, built on the truth of Your Word.
Place us exactly where You want us so we can best reflect You.
We want to build up others and not tear people down.
Help Your people...Your house, to be faithful and strong.
Renew in Your household a spirit of perseverance.
Help us to fix our thoughts on Jesus who gives us hope and courage.

But Christ is faithful as a son over God's house. And we are his house, if we hold on to our courage and the hope of which we boast. (Heb. 3:6)

Enjoy His presence: still yourself, listen, write

January 19

The Door of Deliverance

Father, thank You for Jesus.
He is the Door of deliverance.
He is the Only Way by which we are saved.
Through Him, we not only have eternal life, but we also can have peace and joy in the middle of our struggles and pain.
Thank You, Father, that Your Word exposes lies.
The truth of Your Word is freeing.
You say to ask, seek and knock.
Help us to ask for God's will...and expect to receive.
Create in us a desire to seek more and more of the truth...and expect to find.
Enable us to persist in prayer...and expect the door to be opened.
Holy Spirit, we ask that You use this prayer to knock the door of deliverance open for those who are afflicted and oppressed.

For everyone who asks receives; he who seeks finds; and to him who knocks, the door will be opened. (Matt. 7:8)

Enjoy His presence: still yourself, listen, write

Hallelujah! Amen. It is Done.

January 20

The Finger of God

Father, we adore You.

We praise You that Your Hand reached down for us.

Thank You for the nail-scarred Hands of Jesus that are always reaching out to us.

We praise You that with the work of Your fingers You created the universe and formed and shaped us out of dust and clay.

We praise You for Your Power that is present in just one of Your fingers.

Help us, Father, not to be so blinded by our stubbornness that we don't even see the truth.

Open our eyes to see and understand that You are the Master Potter of our lives, and You can bring good from any problem.

Your plan is not to harm us, but to give what is best.

Help us to recognize Your fingerprints in our lives and submit to Your ways.

"O house of Israel, can I not do with you as this potter does?" declares the LORD. "Like clay in the hand of the potter, so are you in my hand, O house of Israel." (Jer. 18:6)

Enjoy His presence: still yourself, listen, write

January 21

Exposure

Father, You see everything.
You don't miss one thing.
You have a Watchful eye.
You are the Light that dispels darkness.
Your Light exposes lies, and replaces lies with the truth.
Holy Spirit, shine Your Light in the areas of our lives that need cleaning.
Expose Your truth.
Make Your truth visible to us.
Help us to accept Your correction.
We want to please You.
Create in each of us a new mind and heart that is filled with Your Light.
We want to be more like Jesus...
Loving,
Peaceful,
Patient,
and Self-controlled.

But everything exposed by the light becomes visible, for it is light that makes everything visible. (Eph. 5:13-14)

Enjoy His presence: still yourself, listen, write

Hallelujah! Amen. It is Done.

January 22

Like Peter

Father, Your Grace is available everyday, all day.
You understand us.
You know all our limitations and weaknesses and the ugliness in our lives.
Yet, like Peter, when You look on Your children, You see the Blood of Jesus that covers us.
Your Grace is...
forever,
amazing,
and sufficient.
It strengthens,
gives hope,
heals,
protects,
and forgives.
Thank You, Father, for Your tender concern for the brokenhearted.
Thank You for being near and never leaving us.
You give to us, like You gave to Your disciple Peter...
Your transforming Power,
Your Grace,
and the good news of Your Word.

"Don't be alarmed," he said. "You are looking for Jesus the Nazarene, who was crucified. He has risen! He is not here. See the place where they laid him. But go, tell his disciples and Peter, 'He is going ahead of you into Galilee. There you will see him, just as he told you.' " (Mark 16:6-7)

Enjoy His presence: still yourself, listen, write

January 23

Valued

Our Father, words cannot express Your Love for us.
Your Love is unconditional.
You value us in ways our minds cannot fully understand.
Your Love will never change.
When we fall short, You pick us back up again.
We are valued by You because we are Your children.
We belong to Your family because we chose to turn from our sins, and place our faith in Jesus as our Savior and Lord.
We accept Your free Gift of grace.
Holy Spirit, remind us each day that Your heart is True.
You will never...
leave us,
exchange us,
or sell us.
We are valued.
We are Yours!

For you created my inmost being; you knit me together in my mother's womb. I praise you because I am fearfully and wonderfully made; your works are wonderful, I know that full well. (Psalm 139:13-14)

Enjoy His presence: still yourself, listen, write

Hallelujah! Amen. It is Done.

January 24

Living Hope

O Lord, thank You so much for being our Shield of protection.
Thank You, Jesus, for Your Holy Spirit that lives within us.
He is the Power in our lives.
Come and fill us up with a fresh awareness of Your presence.
Remind us often that distractions in our lives are just that.
When things fall apart, we still have hope.
Help us to stand strong for You, because...
You are the Door,
our Protective Screen,
and our Filter.
You are the One True God...our Living Hope.

Praise be to the God and Father of our Lord Jesus Christ! In his great mercy he has given us new birth into a living hope through the resurrection of Jesus Christ from the dead. (1 Peter 1:3)

Enjoy His presence: still yourself, listen, write

Servants

We praise You Father for Your Grace.

Thank You for Your Only Son, Jesus…the True Servant.

Jesus is our covering that surrounds us.

Thank You for protecting us.

Thank You for covering our feelings and sensitive areas of our lives.

Make us strong servants as we follow You.

Desensitize us from anything that would hurt us or get on our nerves.

Enable us to be the servants You've called us to be.

Thank You, Holy Spirit, for Your covering as we serve Your Grace to others.

And you also are among those who are called to belong to Jesus Christ. (Rom. 1:6)

Enjoy His presence: still yourself, listen, write

January 26

Salt

Thank You, Father, for never changing.
Everything about You is the same yesterday, today, and even tomorrow.
You are the necessary Preservative.
Keep us fresh and full of Your Spirit.
Help us to bring out the best in each other.
Take from us, Lord, anything that would dim Your reflection within us.
Humble us and cleanse us, Lord Jesus.
Expose any impurities in us.
Faithful Father, preserve us.

You are the salt of the earth. But if the salt loses its saltiness, how can it be made salty again? It is no longer good for anything, except to be thrown out and trampled by men. (Matt. 5:13)

Enjoy His presence: still yourself, listen, write

January 27

Praying

Jesus, thank You for always praying for us.
Thank You for the awesome privilege of praying with You.
Your Grace makes it possible to come before a Holy God.
Thank You for the Power of prayer.
Thank You for the Power of Your Word in prayer.
Thank You for giving us prayer as a weapon against the enemy.
When we pray, we carry each other to Jesus.
Through prayer, the Holy Spirit of Jesus...
strengthens us,
lifts burdens,
and encourages us.
Help us to always pray for each other.

And pray in the Spirit on all occasions with all kinds of prayers and requests. With this in mind, be alert and always keep on praying for all the saints. (Eph. 6:18)

Enjoy His presence: still yourself, listen, write

Hallelujah! Amen. It is Done.

January 28

Invitation to Come

O God, pour out Your Spirit upon us.
Bring change.
Relight Your fire.
Bring revival.
Renew us.
Refresh us.
Breathe on us.
Cleanse us.
Make us holy.
We need You.
We want Your presence.
We invite You to come.
Come quickly!

When you send your Spirit, they are created, and you renew the face of the earth. (Psalm 104:30)

Enjoy His presence: still yourself, listen, write

My People

Father God, You are Faithful in the tough times and in the good times.
You always look after Your people.
You've brought us through so much.
We thank You for never, ever, leaving us.
We praise You for Your covenant Love.
You always keep Your promises.
Your Victorious Hand is upon Your "Bride".
Remind us that Your grip is tight and nothing can separate us from Your Love.
Remind us of our inheritance, which is ours through Jesus Christ.
Strengthen our faith in the days to come.

"But as for me and my household, we will serve the LORD."
(Joshua 24:15)

Enjoy His presence: still yourself, listen, write

Hallelujah! Amen. It is Done.

January 30

J E S U S

Jesus, we lift our souls in praise to You.
You are the Beginning,
Middle,
and the End.
You are...
the Truth,
the Way,
and the Life.
You are the Good Shepherd,
the Lamb of God,
and King of Kings.
Thank You for Your covenant Love.
Thank You for calling us friend.
Thank You for being a speaking God.
Give us a quickness to discern Your voice.
You speak to us through the pages of the Holy Bible.
Free us, Lord Jesus, to hear Your Word and know Your heart.

The LORD came and stood there, calling as at the other times, "Samuel! Samuel!" Then Samuel said, "Speak, for your servant is listening." (1 Sam. 3:10)

Enjoy His presence: still yourself, listen, write

Three Peas in a Pod

Loving Father, thank You for creating the sacred union of marriage.
Help us to place Jesus in the center of our marriage.
Thank You for the holiness and strength of a Christian marriage, a life together in His presence.
Help us to love our spouse with a Love like Yours...
committed,
never-ending,
and willing to sacrifice.
Humble us, Lord, in our relationships.
May we grow old together with a surrendered heart.
Cover and surround our marriages.
Help husbands and wives live their married lives with You in the center...
like three peas in a pod.

Humble yourselves, therefore, under God's mighty hand, that he may lift you up in due time. (1 Peter 5:6)

Enjoy His presence: still yourself, listen, write

Hallelujah! Amen. It is Done.

February

Photo by Cheryl Fairfield

Praise Him...*Hallelujah!*
Surrender to His will...*Amen.*
Live in faith as His plan unfolds...*It is done.*

February 1

Kisses for Jesus

We lift up the Name of Jesus.
We worship Him.
We adore Him.
He is worthy of our praise.
You are...
our Savior,
our Lord,
our Teacher,
and Friend.
We love You.
Help us to look at You and not ourselves.
We want a close, personal, deep relationship with Jesus.
Help us to spend time with You and get to know You more and more each day.
We love You.
You never get tired of hearing us say..."We love You, Jesus."
Just like we never get tired of You whispering in our hearts... "I love you."
As an act of love and adoration, may our prayers be like kisses on Your feet.

You did not give me a kiss, but this woman, from the time I entered, has not stopped kissing my feet. (Luke 7:45)

Enjoy His presence: still yourself, listen, write

Hallelujah! Amen. It is Done.

February 2

The Truth

Faithful Father, You are the Beginning and the End.
You are the Truth.
You cannot lie.
You say what You mean and mean what You say.
You said that Jesus is...
the Way,
the Truth,
and the Life.
There is no other gospel of grace.
Guard us against false teachings and confusion.
Help us to recognize...
the lie,
the decoy,
the counterfeit.
Holy Spirit, we invite You to breathe the truth into our minds and hearts.
May we accept the truth...the gospel of Jesus Christ.

"You are a king, then!" said Pilate. Jesus answered, "You are right in saying I am a king. In fact, for this reason I was born, and for this I came into the world, to testify to the truth. Everyone on the side of truth listens to me." (John 18:37)

Enjoy His presence: still yourself, listen, write

February 3

I Can't, But He Can

Jesus, You are all about freedom.
You are the means of escape from death.
You are the Key to eternal life.
You are the Power needed to overcome sin.
You are the Master Potter who shapes and molds our lives.
You enable us to live in peace and joy, even in the middle of incredible hardships.
When we sincerely choose to turn from our sins, and in faith, trust You as our Savior and Lord, we are in Christ.
No matter what our handicaps are, or how weak we feel, You are...our Strength.
You are the Power that enables us to grow.
Each day may we grow stronger and closer to You.
May Your Spirit guide us and flow through us.

I can do everything through him who gives me strength.
(Phil. 4:13)

Enjoy His presence: still yourself, listen, write

Hallelujah! Amen. It is Done.

February 4

Constrain

Almighty God, You are the One who holds back evil.
Your Power is greater than any other power in this world.
You are Great, O God.
You are the Champion.
You are the Winner.
Jesus is the One who restrains and knocks down our enemy.
In the Name of Jesus constrain evil.
We thank You for...
what You've done,
are doing,
and will do.

My prayer is not that you take them out of the world but that you protect them from the evil one. (John 17:15)

Enjoy His presence: still yourself, listen, write

February 5

Always Available

Our Father, thank You for always being available.
You are never too busy for us.
You never get in a hurry.
And, You're always willing to listen.
You desire a personal, deep relationship with us.
Take away those things that distract us and lead us away from You.
Strengthen our faith.
Help us to run to You in prayer during the good times and the bad times because... You are always available.

"Call to me and I will answer you and tell you great and unsearchable things you do not know." (Jer. 33:3)

Enjoy His presence: still yourself, listen, write

Hallelujah! Amen. It is Done.

February 6

Before and After

Our Father, thank You for constantly loving us and protecting us.
You are always on the alert, watching out for us.
You never leave us.
Our faith in Jesus shields us.
You go before us and after us.
You guide us.
You are our Rear Guard.
You never sleep or look the other way.
You are Ever-Present.

For the LORD will go before you, the God of Israel will be your rear guard. (Isaiah 52:12)

Enjoy His presence: still yourself, listen, write

February 7

Follow the Leader

Lord Jesus, You are the One True God.
You always were and always will be.
You are the Leader.
We want You to be first in our lives: first in our...
marriages,
jobs,
friendships,
money,
and with our children.
We want to follow You.
Help us to recognize evidence of Your presence as we walk this journey.
Increase our trust in You, as we follow Your lead.

Trust in the LORD forever, for the LORD, the LORD, is the Rock eternal. (Isaiah 26:4)

Enjoy His presence: still yourself, listen, write

Hallelujah! Amen. It is Done.

February 8

Guidance

Sweet Spirit, thank You for Your Wisdom and Power.
Thank You for protecting us.
Help us to look to You for guidance.
Your Word...
counsels,
directs,
convicts,
and encourages.
Forgive us when we try to do things without even consulting You.
Open our minds and hearts to Your truth, so we can clearly discern Your leading.
We surrender our wills to You, O God, because Your Right Hand guides us.

I will praise the LORD, who counsels me; even at night my heart instructs me. I have set the LORD always before me. Because he is at my right hand, I will not be shaken.
(Psalm 16:7-8)

Enjoy His presence: still yourself, listen, write

Dance with the Lord

Father God, You are the Creator of All.
You are the Gift Giver.
You created the union of marriage.
First, may husbands and wives respond to Your call to come closer to You.
Next, bring husbands and wives closer to each other.
Remove anything that wants to get between them and pull them apart.
Help them to cling to You.
Empower them to choose to focus on the positive traits of their spouses.
Help them to intentionally take the time to spend enjoyable times together.
Bless them with laughter, fun, and romantic moments.

Rejoice in the Lord always. I will say it again: Rejoice! Let your gentleness be evident to all. The Lord is near.
(Phil. 4:4-5)

Enjoy His presence: still yourself, listen, write

Hallelujah! Amen. It is Done.

February 10

Working

Our Father, thank You for creating our bodies like You did.
You formed us in such wonderful ways.
Your design is so intricate.
Each part of the body is wonderfully made: the heart, the brain,
the eye, the ear.
Guard our bodies, minds, and hearts.
We want to grow stronger and closer to You.
Thank You for all our abilities.
May we use our bodies to glorify You.
Help us to come together in peace and work together using
our strengths, talents,
and gifts from You...for You.

***Whatever you do, work at it with all your heart, as working
for the Lord, not for men.*** (Col. 3:23)

Enjoy His presence: still yourself, listen, write

February 11

Fullness in You

Lord, You are the Giver of Joy.
You want us to have Your Peace.
Your Peace guards the way we think and feel.
You want us to experience life to the fullest.
Help us to seek a deeper relationship with You.
Even when we walk through long, difficult times, may we have that inner peace that whispers in our heart…"Everything is going to be okay."
Help us to be attentive to You and watch for You throughout our day.
Turn our eyes directly to Jesus so we may accept and receive all the blessings we have through Him.

I have come so that they may have life and have it to the full. (John 10:10)

Enjoy His presence: still yourself, listen, write

Hallelujah! Amen. It is Done.

February 12

Commit Yourself

Faithful Father, may Your will be done.
You are God Most High.
We can trust You.
We can rest in Your ways.
We surrender to Your plan.
We want You to direct our paths.
Check our hearts for pure motives.
Help us to remember whom we are serving.
Humble us Lord, as we receive Your blessings as we serve others.
Each day may we trust You even more.
May we be reminded often that our power and blessings come from You.
Jesus, the Risen Lord, we commit ourselves to You!

Commit to the LORD whatever you do, and your plans will succeed. (Proverbs 16:3)

Enjoy His presence: still yourself, listen, write

February 13

Evil Is Contained

Almighty God, nothing in heaven and on earth can contain You.
You are Unlimited.
You are Number One.
You are God Most High.
Thank You, Father, for sending us Jesus.
He has paid the full price for each one of us.
Jesus has contained evil for those who repent of their sins, and place their faith in Him.
Thank You, Father, for reminding us as many times as we need, that we don't have to be afraid...Jesus has taken care of everything.
Each second and every day of our lives is known and prayed for by Jesus.
We are His treasures.
We are His property.
Holy Spirit, thank You for Your Power in us that enables us to overcome.

Who is it that overcomes the world? Only he who believes that Jesus is the Son of God. (1 John 5:5)

Enjoy His presence: still yourself, listen, write

Hallelujah! Amen. It is Done.

February 14

Little Children, Come

Mighty Father, You love children.
We bring to You in prayer the children who are walking through dark times of...
fear,
loneliness,
neglect,
or abandonment.
Soothe their fears.
Guard them from people who have harmful intentions.
Send someone to tell them about the Hope we have in Jesus.
Help them to walk directly to Your Light.
May these precious children...
accept Jesus,
trust Him,
and grow in Him.
You used children to teach adults about trust and childlike faith.
Thank You for extending Your arms and blessing the children.
May all come as little children to Jesus.

"Let the little children come to me, and do not hinder them, for the kingdom of God belongs to such as these."
And he took the children in his arms, put his hands on them and blessed them. (Mark 10:14, 16)

Enjoy His presence: still yourself, listen, write

February 15

Quick to Listen

Loving Father, we praise You, because You are quick to listen.
You Love us.
You are Steady and Sure.
What a comfort it is to know that You are always willing to listen to us.
Help us to be quick to listen to You.
Create in us a discipline to quiet ourselves and listen to You speak to us through the pages of the Bible.
Help us to be quick to listen to others, even when we have lots to do.
Slow us down.
Help us not to jump from one thing to another.
Enable us to stop what we're doing and listen to people.
Touch our spiritual hearing, as well as our physical hearing, so we can effectively listen to You and Your people.
We need You.
Empower us to be quick to listen.

My dear brothers, take note of this: Everyone should be quick to listen, slow to speak and slow to become angry. (James 1:19)

Enjoy His presence: still yourself, listen, write

Hallelujah! Amen. It is Done.

February 16

The Voices of Brides

O Father, Thank You for Jesus.
Thank You that He is at Your right Hand constantly praying for us.
Holy Spirit, empower us with the discipline it takes to pray.
Deliver us from busyness.
Free us from feeling that our prayers are inadequate.
May we be a nation of prayer.
May we choose to repent and pray.
May our prayers be like the voices of brides waiting for Jesus to come.
We want Your Bride, the Church, to be a house of prayer.
Help us to pray as we wait for the Bridegroom....Jesus.
Thank You for hearing our prayers.

A voice of one calling: "In the desert prepare the way for the LORD; make straight in the wilderness a highway for our God." (Isaiah 40:3)

Enjoy His presence: still yourself, listen, write

Games

Father, You know everything.
You know all about us.
You know the truth.
Free us from playing games with You.
We cannot "con" God.
Touch our strong wills and forgive our stubbornness.
Create in us a deep hunger to know You more.
Change our minds by knowing the truth of Your Word.
Change our stubbornness to submissiveness to Your way.
You are LORD God.

O LORD, you have searched me and you know me. You know when I sit and when I rise; you perceive my thoughts from afar. You discern my going out and my lying down; you are familiar with all my ways. (Psalm 139:1-3)

Enjoy His presence: still yourself, listen, write

Hallelujah! Amen. It is Done.

February 18

Embrace

Father, Your Love is everlasting.
Your Love is steady and sure.
Thank You for loving us so much that You gave Your Only Son as a ransom for our sins.
Thank You, Jesus, for Your arms that are always open for us.
You stretched out Your arms and died for us.
May we respond to Your grace.
Help us to allow You to embrace us with Your Power and Comfort.
May we feel Your Compassion and everlasting Love surrounding us.
Thank You for Your presence and strong hold on us.
May we lean in, and allow ourselves to be embraced by Jesus.

The eternal God is our refuge, and underneath are the everlasting arms. (Deu. 33:27)

Enjoy His presence: still yourself, listen, write

February 19

Safe

Jesus, You are a protective Shield around us.
Your Power is supernatural.
You are greater than any other power in this world.
You are Sovereign.
You are Almighty.
You fight for us.
We can rest in Your shadow.
Your Name brings the enemy down.
Let us run to Jesus and be safe.

The name of the LORD is a strong tower; the righteous run to it and are safe. (Prov. 18:10)

Enjoy His presence: still yourself, listen, write

Hallelujah! Amen. It is Done.

February 20

Lifeline

Lord Jesus, Your saving love is our Lifeline.
You are the Only One who gives eternal life.
You are the source of all growth.
We want to grow deeper in love with You.
We want to mature.
You are all the ingredients for an abundant life.
You are...
the Joy Giver,
the Prince of Peace,
and the Balance in our lives.
Help us to be more and more like You.
Forgive us of selfishness and pride.
Your Holy Spirit enables us to overcome sin.
As You shape and mold us, help us to hold onto You...our Lifeline.

Salvation is found in no one else, for there is no other name under heaven given to men by which we must be saved.
(Acts 4:12)

Enjoy His presence: still yourself, listen, write

February 21

Crushed

Dearest Jesus, thank You that You paid the price for our sins.
Your body was crushed for us.
You took death on the cross so we could have life.
Remind us everyday that the grave could not hold You.
You are alive today.
You give the Power to overcome.
Send Your Spirit to those who are addicted to alcohol.
In the Name of Jesus, crush that addiction.
Free their minds with the Power of Jesus.
May they walk in Your Victory.

**The LORD is close to the brokenhearted and saves those
who are crushed in spirit.** (Psalm 34:18)

Enjoy His presence: still yourself, listen, write

Hallelujah! Amen. It is Done.

February 22

Leave Her Alone

Father, we praise You for being Fair.
This world is not Fair, but You are.
Jesus died for all people.
You take up for, and fight for, both men and women.
You are mindful of...
the least likely,
the underdog,
the mistreated,
and the misunderstood.
We thank You for protecting us.
You have won the battle for us and given us the full armor of God.
Thank You for praying for us...right now.

"Leave her alone," said Jesus. (Mark 14:6)

Enjoy His presence: still yourself, listen, write

February 23

Two

Loving Father, You created the union of marriage and made it holy.
You created each partner with special gifts and talents.
You made a man and a woman as a gift to one another.
Empower husbands and wives to encourage one another.
Help married couples keep their focus on Jesus.
His Forgiveness and Power can hold husbands and wives together.
Take away from husbands and wives whatever it is that keeps them from…
loving unselfishly,
serving each other,
and praying together.
May the two be a powerful team for You.

Dear friends, let us love one another, for love comes from God. (1 John 4:7)

Enjoy His presence: still yourself, listen, write

Hallelujah! Amen. It is Done.

February 24

Childlike Faith

Jesus, You are the Messiah.
You are the True King.
There is none like You.
You are Genuine,
Real,
and Alive today.
Help us to recognize quickly what is not of You.
Help us to see the counterfeit or fake.
Open our minds and hearts to believe that what You say is true.
Holy Spirit, open eyes so we may recognize Jesus, and place our faith in Him.
Give us a childlike faith.
Jesus is Lord and Savior of the world!

And he said: "I tell you the truth, unless you change and become like little children, you will never enter the kingdom of heaven." (Matt. 18:3)

Enjoy His presence: still yourself, listen, write

February 25

Ordering Angels

Father God, You are the Authority over all.
You command the angels.
They take orders from You...Most High God.
Thank You for Your utmost protection.
Thank You for loving us the way You do.
Press in our minds that even though we may feel overwhelmed
and out of control...You are in control.
You have Your Mighty army surrounding us.
You are the Commander of All.

***For he will command his angels concerning you to guard
you in all your ways.*** (Psalm 91:11)

Enjoy His presence: still yourself, listen, write

Hallelujah! Amen. It is Done.

February 26

Make Us Ready

Father, You are the Master Potter.
You shape and mold our lives.
You want the very best for us.
Help us not to fight Your Hands.
Give us a deep desire to know You more.
Give us patience during times of waiting.
Help us to yield to Your plan and timing.
Even during "drying" times, as we wait on You, it's not wasted time.
You have a purpose for our waiting.
Prepare us, Lord, and make our faith stronger.
Help us to trust You, as You make us ready for the next season in our lives.

Wait for the LORD; be strong and take heart and wait for the LORD. (Psalm 27:14)

Enjoy His presence: still yourself, listen, write

February 27

Stronghold

Jesus, You are the Stronghold in a believer's life.
Your right Hand holds us all day long.
You care deeply about us.
You love us.
You watch us with the greatest attention, as we go in and out of difficult times.
You see it all.
You know everything.
You are permanently with us.
We cannot be snatched out of Your Hand.
We love You, Jesus.
Thank You for Your Strong hold on us.

Yet I am always with you; you hold me by my right hand.
(Psalm 73:23)

Enjoy His presence: still yourself, listen, write

Hallelujah! Amen. It is Done.

February 28

More

Father, thank You for Jesus.
He is more than enough.
He is exactly like You.
Thank You for loving us so much that You gave us the Gift of Your Son.
We need Jesus.
He died for our sins.
When we turn from our sins and place our faith in Jesus, we are free from God's wrath.
You want us to live with You forevermore.
Open eyes to recognize the truth about Jesus...Our Redeemer.
Help us, Lord, not to get stuck in our unworthiness.
Instead, help us to accept Jesus...Your Gift of grace.
Release in us Your Power to reach out and receive all that You desire for us.
Let us not be satisfied with less.
Let us seek the One who blesses abundantly more!

The thief comes only to steal and kill and destroy; I have come that they may have life, and have it to the full. (John 10:10)

Enjoy His presence: still yourself, listen, write

February 29 (leap year)

Our Heart

Father, Your Love…
never changes,
never gets in a hurry,
always listens,
and is willing to sacrifice.
You are…
Loyal,
Zealous,
and Kind.
Open our hearts so we may grow to a deeper understanding
of Your great Love.
We don't want to be satisfied to know just a little bit about You.
Help us to know You in our hearts, not just in our heads.
Fill us with the desire to know more about Your Love and who
we are because of our faith in Jesus Christ.
You are worthy of all our love.

And I pray that you, being rooted and established in love,
may have power, together with all the saints, to grasp how
wide and long and high and deep is the love of Christ,
and to know this love that surpasses knowledge--- that
you may be filled to the measure of all the fullness of God.
(Eph. 3:17-19)

Enjoy His presence: still yourself, listen, write

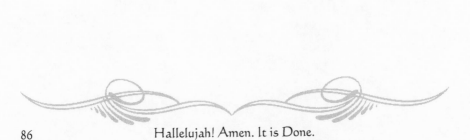

Hallelujah! Amen. It is Done.

March

Photo by Jennifer Taylor

Praise Him…*Hallelujah!*
Surrender to His will…*Amen.*
Live in faith as His plan unfolds…*It is done.*

March 1

Flex

Father, You are Trustworthy.
You are Faithful and keep all Your promises.
Help us to flex and bend according to Your will.
Help us not to resist where You're calling us.
Forgive us when our hearts are stiff and stubborn.
Help us to become more aware of the times when we try to muscle things in our own strength.
Jesus, You are the Lord of our lives.
We want You to...
control,
drive,
and lead us according to Your way.

"Be still, and know that I am God." (Psalm 46:10)

Enjoy His presence: still yourself, listen, write

Hallelujah! Amen. It is Done.

March 2

Watchful Eye

We praise You, Lord, for protecting us in ways we're not even aware.
You see everybody.
You see everything going on.
Remind us that You are still Good even when things happen to us that are not good.
You care about us, no matter what our situation.
Our troubles have passed through Your heart, too.
You are Faithful.
You are a Shield around us.
Lord God, thanks for loving us more than we can ever imagine.
Your Watchful eye is forever upon us.

The eyes of the LORD are everywhere, keeping watch on the wicked and the good. (Prov. 15:3)

Enjoy His presence: still yourself, listen, write

March 3

Stand in the Middle

Father God, You never get in a hurry with us.
You bring calmness.
You give peace.
You are Perfect.
You are the Help we need to balance things in our lives.
Give us the wisdom to say, "no" when needed, and "yes" when needed.
Empower us to set boundaries in our lives.
Remove distractions and lies that come up in our day.
Open our eyes so we can clearly see where Your beam of balance is in our lives.
Help us to seek the Truth.
May we stand in the middle of Your Perfect balance.

Stand firm then, with the belt of truth buckled around your waist, with the breastplate of righteousness in place. (Eph. 6:14)

Enjoy His presence: still yourself, listen, write

Hallelujah! Amen. It is Done.

March 4

Deeper Relationship

Holy Spirit, we love You.
We worship You.
We want You.
Forgive us of our prideful attitudes.
We need You.
Holy Spirit, create in us the desire and discipline to seek You more and more.
Deepen our relationship with Jesus.
Increase and intensify our desire to grow closer to Him.
We want to reflect the Light of Jesus to others.
Come, Holy Spirit, and create in us a burning love for Jesus.

Jesus replied: "Love the Lord your God with all your heart and with all your soul and with all your mind." (Matt. 22:37)

Enjoy His presence: still yourself, listen, write

New Life

Jesus, You are the Gift to us from the Father.
You are the Gift of Everlasting Life.
Repenting of our sins and placing our faith in Jesus as our Savior
and Lord puts our name in the Lamb's Book of Life.
Father, You are the Winner.
We know the judgment has been announced concerning the
evil one.
We ask that You neutralize him so people may see and hear
the Truth.
Push back confusion and lies about Jesus.
Stop the enemy from deceiving us.
Help us to clearly recognize the lies of the enemy.
Jesus, we praise You for constantly interceding for us.
We proclaim Your victory over death, and Your gift of new life.

**For the wages of sin is death, but the gift of God is eternal
life in Christ Jesus our Lord.** (Rom. 6:23)

Enjoy His presence: still yourself, listen, write

Hallelujah! Amen. It is Done.

March 6

Quickly Forgiven

Gracious Father, thank You for Your unconditional Love.
Your Love never changes and lasts forever.
You are a Holy God.
Thank You for loving us so much that You gave us Your Son, Jesus...the Only Way to You.
He paid in full the price for our sins.
When we turn from our sins and place our faith in Him, we are forever forgiven.
You quickly forgive and forget.
You don't keep score.
You cover us with the righteousness of Jesus.
Remind us often that we are forgiven through the Blood of Jesus Christ.
Nothing can change Your Truth.

God made him who had no sin to be sin for us, so that in him we might become the righteousness of God. (2 Cor. 5:21)

Enjoy His presence: still yourself, listen, write

March 7

The Answer

Jesus is the Answer to all our...
questions,
struggles,
hurts,
and anxieties.
He is our Hope.
He will...
guide us,
protect us,
help us,
comfort us,
care for us,
and never leave our side.
Holy Spirit, enlighten our minds and hearts.
Bring us to the truth about the Messiah, Jesus Christ.
He is the Answer.

"Yes, Lord," she told him, "I believe that you are the Christ, the Son of God, who was to come into the world." (John 11:27)

Enjoy His presence: still yourself, listen, write

Hallelujah! Amen. It is Done.

March 8

The Door

Jesus, Savior and Lord...You are the Door.
You point the Only Way to the entrance to eternal life.
Through repentance and placing our faith in You, the door is flung wide open.
What You open no one can shut.
Your right Hand is upon us.
You hear our prayers.
You take care of us.
You supply all that we need.
You are the Door through which we receive free, abundant life.

I am the gate; whoever enters through me will be saved.
(John 10:9)

Enjoy His presence: still yourself, listen, write

March 9

Holy Fire

Father God, You are Holy.
Thank You for Jesus, the Precious Lamb of God.
He became the Perfect Sacrifice for our sins.
Thank You that we can have a personal relationship with Him
when we repent and believe.
You are alive.
You go ahead of us.
You are protecting us and comforting us as You guide us along
the way.
Thank You for Your presence in our lives.
Thank You for reassuring us with the truth of Your Word.
Your Holy Word burns away those things in our hearts that are
displeasing to You.
Teach us and refine us in Your Holy Fire.
Make us more like You.

**But be assured today that the LORD your God is the one
who goes across ahead of you like a devouring fire.**
(Deu. 9:3)

Enjoy His presence: still yourself, listen, write

Hallelujah! Amen. It is Done.

March 10

All Calm

Father, Your Love is everlasting.
We praise You and thank You for Your sustaining Power.
Your Hand is constantly reaching out to us.
Your ear is always attentive to us.
You hear our prayers.
Thank You for pulling us through the storms in our lives.
You are the Power that calms us.
Help us, Lord, to rest in Your strength.
Remind us that we can have joy in the middle of the storm.
You are the Joy-Giver.
You are the Prince of Peace.
You have us in Your Hand.
We are Yours.
You make everything okay.

I call on the LORD in my distress, and he answers me.
(Psalm 120:1)

Enjoy His presence: still yourself, listen, write

God's Order

Great God, You like order.
You created the universe and placed all things in order.
Your Divine order is evident in our...
bodies,
families,
and government.
You are the Great I AM.
You are in control even when things seem out of control.
Help us to give every part of our lives to Jesus.
He will order our footsteps, one step at a time.
Great God, mold and shape us according to Your order...step by step, piece by piece.

"How great you are, O Sovereign LORD! There is no one like you, and there is no God but you, as we have heard with our own ears." (2 Sam. 7:22)

Enjoy His presence: still yourself, listen, write

Hallelujah! Amen. It is Done.

March 12

The Wall

Almighty Father, You are the Wall that protects us.
Your Love surrounds us.
Your Blood covers us.
We may see and hear the evil attack, but You can deflect any scheme of the devil.
Jesus can tear down walls of hurt in our hearts and minds.
He has given us the victory over evil.
Help us not to be afraid.
Help us to live with an awareness of Your wall of protection around us.
We praise You…Almighty Father.

As the mountains surround Jerusalem, so the LORD surrounds his people both now and forevermore. (Psalm 125:2)

Enjoy His presence: still yourself, listen, write

Pierce

Father, Your Grace is unlimited.
Your Grace never runs out.
Words do not adequately express our gratitude for Your saving Grace.
Holy Spirit, pierce hearts with the tender message of God's Grace through Jesus Christ.
Through Him we are forgiven and have eternal life.
Soften hearts and change minds.
Take away any hardening or toughness in our emotions and thinking.
May we accept and receive the One who was pierced for us.
Jesus is the Savior for all and the Lord of all.

But he was pierced for our transgressions, he was crushed for our iniquities; the punishment that brought us peace was upon him, and by his wounds we are healed. (Isaiah 53:5)

Enjoy His presence: still yourself, listen, write

Hallelujah! Amen. It is Done.

March 14

Fan the Flame

Father, we call out in joy, praising You for giving us Jesus.
Create in us a burning desire to know who we are in Christ.
Holy Spirit, we invite You to teach us the ways of Jesus.
Set each believer on fire with a teachable spirit so they develop
and use their unique gift of God.
We want our gift from God to burn brightly in our…
homes,
work places,
churches,
communities,
and the world.
Ignite us with Your Power.

For this reason I remind you to fan into flame the gift of God, which is in you through the laying on of my hands. (2 Tim. 1:6)

Enjoy His presence: still yourself, listen, write

March 15

Extension Rod

Merciful God, we praise You.
You are Almighty.
You have Authority over all.
Your Mercy extends beyond our understanding.
We humbly say thank You for Your redeeming Mercy.
Thank You, Jesus, for extending Your arms and dying for us on the cross.
Your outstretched Hands bring eternal comfort.
Our souls cry out in gratitude.
We sing praises to You for extending to us fresh Mercy each day.
Guide and protect us.
We love You.
We bow to You.

His mercy extends to those who fear Him, from generation to generation. (Luke 1:50)

Enjoy His presence: still yourself, listen, write

Hallelujah! Amen. It is Done.

March 16

The Best Way

Jesus, thank You for Your way.
Your way is the best way, even if we don't agree or understand.
You are God, and we are not.
You know the "big picture."
You always have our best interests in mind.
Your Love is unconditional and everlasting.
You know what it takes for our love to grow deeper, and our faith to grow stronger.
You've given us powerful ingredients to promote growth...
Bible study,
prayer,
Christian fellowship,
and worship.
All these ingredients help our love to grow deeper, and our faith to grow stronger.
Help us to respond to Your call to grow.
Sanctify us according to Your pace and Your plan.

"For I know the plans I have for you," declares the LORD, "plans to prosper you and not to harm you, plans to give you hope and a future." (Jer. 29:11)

Enjoy His presence: still yourself, listen, write

March 17

The Art of Marriage

Father, You created the union of a man and a woman in marriage.
Holy Spirit, guide and strengthen our marriages.
Lead us to a closer, deeper relationship with Jesus.
He can bring married couples closer together.
Help husbands and wives to pray together.
Release in us any lie that would keep married couples from praying together.
Lord, teach us those qualities that bring peace and harmony in a marriage.
Teach us…
to forgive,
to listen,
and to think positive thoughts about our spouses.
Increase our love for one another, as we stay focused on You.
We want Jesus to be the Artist of our marriage, shaping and molding us together with Him.

"Like clay in the hand of the potter, so are you in my hand, O house of Israel." (Jer. 18:6)

Enjoy His presence: still yourself, listen, write

Hallelujah! Amen. It is Done.

March 18

P R A Y

Father, we thank You and praise You for this remarkable privilege of prayer.

Jesus is our Great Intercessor.

We praise You for Your Power, which is released when Your children come together and pray in agreement with Your will.

Help us to persevere in prayer.

You use persistent prayer to knock down walls in minds and hearts.

Help us not to get discouraged as we wait on You.

Fill us with Your Joy.

Thank You for hearing our prayers.

Pray continually; give thanks in all circumstances, for this is God's will for you in Christ Jesus. (1 Thess. 5:17-18)

Enjoy His presence: still yourself, listen, write

March 19

Desensitize

Loving Father, You give us more than enough.
You give us what we need according to Your glorious riches in Jesus.
Your One and Only Son is Everything and then more.
Remind us that as we follow You and spread the good news of the gospel, You are with us every step of the way.
You walk right beside us.
Push back distractions throughout our day, so we can sense Your presence.
When we get tired, desensitize our weary souls and bring strength.
When we suffer, desensitize our pain and bring relief.
You never said life in this world would be easy or free from struggles.
But Your Word assures us that You can bring good from the not-so-good.
Help us to walk with boldness and courage as we live our lives for Jesus.
Thank You for hearing our prayers.
Your blessings are upon us.

As it is written, "How beautiful are the feet of those who bring good news!" (Rom. 10:15)

Enjoy His presence: still yourself, listen, write

Hallelujah! Amen. It is Done.

March 20

Submit

Jesus, You are Lord God.
You are God Most High.
Forgive us for being stubborn and wanting our own way.
Open our hands so we don't hold on to old hurts.
Give us Your Comfort when we are...
unfairly treated,
misunderstood,
or ignored.
Remind us that You know.
Help us to trust You and humbly come before You with our hurts.
In a spirit of brokenness help us to submit our situation to You.
You are the Power that can change things.
We choose to follow You.
Enable us to mutually submit to one another because we love You.

Submit to one another out of reverence for Christ. (Eph. 5:21)

Enjoy His presence: still yourself, listen, write

March 21

Bubbles

Praise You, Jesus, because ultimately, everything is going to be okay.
You have prayed for us.
You're in charge.
Your Word reassures us that You will take care of all our needs.
We are all different.
We are fragile.
We can easily fall apart.
Yet each one of us, in some way, captures the reflection of You.
Your Power holds us together.
Thank You for bringing us together in prayer.
You are delighted when we come together, and agree with You.
Together we lift up our...
prayers,
songs,
and services, so we may glorify You.
In joy we celebrate You!

They are a fragrant offering, an acceptable sacrifice, pleasing to God. (Phil. 4:18)

Enjoy His presence: still yourself, listen, write

Hallelujah! Amen. It is Done.

March 22

Good Shepherd

Jesus, we praise You!
We sing for joy because You are the Good Shepherd and we
are Your sheep.
You will provide for us.
You watch over us.
You never take Your eyes off Your sheep.
You will never, ever, leave us.
You are Gracious.
You speak.
Thank You for the awesome privilege of hearing and knowing
Your voice.
Help us to quickly recognize what is noise.
Teach us to listen to You.
Thank You for guiding us and protecting us.
You are...the Good Shepherd.

The LORD is my shepherd, I shall not be in want. (Psalm 23:1)

Enjoy His presence: still yourself, listen, write

March 23

The Way

Thank You, Holy Spirit, for praying for us.
It is a great privilege to join You in prayer.
We stand in awe that You want to include us.
You are Gracious.
Your Word and prayer are mighty weapons against the enemy.
Thank You for giving us Your Word.
Your Word strengthens us.
Your Power enables us to walk through incredibly hard times.
You cover us with Your Protection.
We are more than conquerors.
Jesus unlocks those things that hold us captive.
Jesus sets us free.
He is the Way to a victorious life.

So if the Son sets you free, you will be free indeed. (John 8:36)

Enjoy His presence: still yourself, listen, write

Hallelujah! Amen. It is Done.

March 24

Fitted and Ready

Holy Spirit, send us where You want.
We don't want to go anywhere without You.
You will send us where You have already gone.
We want Your perfect timing.
Guard us from getting ahead of You.
Prepare us and get us ready to tell others about Jesus.
You are the Prince of Peace, therefore, we choose not to be afraid.
We choose to be encouragers.
We want to leave Your Peace with people wherever we go.
We praise You for getting us ready and empowering us to give to others the gospel of peace.

Stand firm then, with the belt of truth buckled around your waist, with the breastplate of righteousness in place, and with your feet fitted with the readiness that comes from the gospel of peace. (Eph. 6:14-15)

Enjoy His presence: still yourself, listen, write

Postpone

Father, Your timing is the best, even when it doesn't feel like it.
You always have our best interests in mind.
Sometimes You answer prayers right away.
Sometimes You answer prayers later.
As we wait on You, help us to feel deep within that everything is going to be okay.
Help us not to worry or fret.
Push back disappointment in Your timing.
Renew our strength as we wait on You.
Remind us that we can trust Your timing.
Our hope is in You.

He has made everything beautiful in its time. (Ecc. 3:11)

Enjoy His presence: still yourself, listen, write

Hallelujah! Amen. It is Done.

March 26

Cut Away

Gracious Father, You are Holy and will not tolerate sin.
Thank You for giving us Jesus.
He is the Only Way back to You.
He is Your plan for our redemption.
He is the One who saves, delivers, and heals.
Holy Spirit, cut away from us those things that rob us of our peace and joy.
Cut away...
lies,
anger,
past hurts,
circular thinking,
harsh words,
and fear.
You have given us the Power of forgiveness.
Remind us that You bring comfort.
You can fix things.
You can restore relationships.
You can guard emotions.
You are able to cut away negative thinking and negative emotions and bring peace to our minds and hearts.

Now to him who is able to do immeasurably more than all we ask or imagine, according to his power that is at work within us, to him be glory in the church and in Christ Jesus throughout all generations, for ever and ever! Amen. (Eph. 3:20-21)

Enjoy His presence: still yourself, listen, write

Visible Garbage

Our Father, we praise You, because through Jesus Christ we are more than conquerors.

His resurrection Power enables us to rise above our present situation.

Jesus is the Truth that sets us free.

Help those that have been hurt deeply, not to keep the hurt deeply hidden.

Because when we speak about the hurt and bring it out into the open, healing can begin.

Remind us that no sin is too big for Jesus' grace to cover.

One drop of His Blood can restore the damage from deep hurts.

Help us not to hide the garbage in our lives.

Instead, help us to allow You to take the garbage out of our lives, and replace that garbage with Your truth and healing.

Then you will know the truth, and the truth will set you free.
(John 8:32)

Enjoy His presence: still yourself, listen, write

Hallelujah! Amen. It is Done.

March 28

Honor God

Loving Father, we want to honor You in all we do.
Our actions are outward reflections of what's inside our hearts.
Father, we bring to Your feet those who participate in physically degrading actions.
Have mercy on those who persistently do vile things.
Send Your Spirit of repentance.
Change minds and hearts.
Help people to develop strong Christ-like morals.
Our bodies are made by You.
Our bodies are made for Your dwelling.
Father, in Jesus' Name, free people from desecrating their bodies.

Flee from sexual immorality. (1 Cor. 6:18)

Enjoy His presence: still yourself, listen, write

March 29

Exchange

Thank You, Father, for Your Gift of Grace.
Help us to exchange worldly things that are temporary, for lasting peace.
Jesus can exchange…
darkness for light,
weakness for strength,
worry for peace,
confusion for clarity,
and death for life.
All praise and glory to Lord Jesus Christ.

But those who hope in the LORD will renew their strength.
They will soar on wings like eagles; they will run and not
grow weary, they will walk and not be faint. (Isaiah 40:31)

Enjoy His presence: still yourself, listen, write

Hallelujah! Amen. It is Done.

March 30

Purify My Heart

Gracious Father, You are getting Your Bride ready for Your return.
We come to You as Your children, waiting to be picked up by Your Only Son, Jesus.
We have not treated You like You deserve.
Forgive us for turning away from Your face.
Bring us back to You, our First Love.
We need You.
Remove in us anything that keeps us from responding to Your invitation to come closer.
Purify us.
Move our hearts in Your direction.
We want our love for You to grow stronger.
May we be devoted to You.
We praise You for Your mercy.

Create in me a pure heart, O God, and renew a steadfast spirit within me. (Psalm 51:10)

Enjoy His presence: still yourself, listen, write

You Are the Elevator

Father, You lift burdens and carry us when we're weak.
You take us to higher ground.
You can lift depression.
You can lift loneliness.
Your resurrection Power is ours through Jesus Christ.
Through Him, we are elevated from death to life.
Help us to drop all our anxieties and burdens on Your shoulders.
You're the One who lifts them away.
We exalt the Name of Jesus.
He is the Rock of our salvation,
the Lifter of our heads,
and worthy of our praise!

He lifted me out of the slimy pit, out of the mud and mire; he set my feet on a rock and gave me a firm place to stand. (Psalm 40:2)

Enjoy His presence: still yourself, listen, write

Hallelujah! Amen. It is Done.

April

Photo by Jennifer Taylor

Praise Him...*Hallelujah!*
Surrender to His will...*Amen.*
Live in faith as His plan unfolds...*It is done.*

April 1

Renewed to Serve

Holy Spirit of God, we praise You for Your transforming Power.
You make things happen.
We praise You for the gracious privilege of praying with You.
You are able to do all things on Your own, but You choose to
include us.
Prayer is powerful when we agree with You.
Holy Spirit, bring to our minds how Jesus modeled the life of a
Humble Servant.
Renew in us a humble attitude to serve others.
Help us to love others like You love us.
Help us to look at others through the eyes of grace.
Take away...
tiredness,
disappointments,
and self-centeredness.
Instill in us...
energy,
joy,
and sacrificial love.
We come in thanksgiving and expectancy, because we know
You hear our prayers.
We thank You now, for what is happening, and will happen in
Your Church.

***Now that I, your Lord and Teacher, have washed your feet,
you also should wash one another's feet. I have set you
an example that you should do as I have done for you.***
(John 13:14-15)

Enjoy His presence: still yourself, listen, write

Hallelujah! Amen. It is Done.

April 2

River of Life

Holy Spirit of God, You are like a river that quenches thirst and restores life.
Draw people to the truth about Jesus.
He is the Living Water.
He is the One who satisfies our thirsty souls.
He is the One who gives everlasting life.
We want to tell others the good news about Jesus.
Enable us to make a difference for You.
We want to stand strong in You.
May Your people come to know Your Mighty Power that is at work within them.
Use us, Lord.

Then the angel showed me the river of the water of life, as clear as crystal, flowing from the throne of God and of the Lamb. (Rev. 22:1)

Enjoy His presence: still yourself, listen, write

April 3

Filling Us...Premium

Holy Spirit, You take care of everything in every way.
You have overcome the world.
Help us not to forget that Your Spirit lives within believers.
Daily fill our minds and hearts with Your Power.
Thank You for giving us the best.
What You give is eternal life, and life to the fullest, now.
You are Most High God.
You are Above All.
There is none like You.
You are Premium.
Come, and fill Your Church!

And God placed all things under his feet and appointed him to be head over everything for the church, which is his body, the fullness of him who fills everything in every way. (Eph. 1:22-23)

Enjoy His presence: still yourself, listen, write

Hallelujah! Amen. It is Done.

April 4

Spots

Gracious Father, thank You for Jesus.
His Blood washes away the stain of sin.
His Blood alone cleanses our spot-stained souls.
He can remove our deepest, darkest sin, in the past or present.
Forgive us, Jesus, and remove spots of…
pride,
lies,
and deep hurts,
by the Power of Your Name.
Guard us from any type of false teachings.
Protect us from any twist or distortion of the Truth.
Jesus is the Only One who can forgive our sins.

***Salvation is found in no one else, for there is no other name
under heaven given to men by which we must be saved.***
(Acts 4:12)

Enjoy His presence: still yourself, listen, write

April 5

Glued to You

Father God, You are what holds us together.
You are Powerful and True.
You are Alive.
You are the Living Word.
Your Word...
saves,
delivers,
guides,
comforts,
and heals.
By the Power of Your Word, keep us close to You.
Help us to stick with You, no matter how tough things get.
Guard us from anything that would want to tear us away from
the truth of Your Word.

*"Every word of God is flawless; he is a shield to those who
take refuge in him."* (Prov. 30:5)

Enjoy His presence: still yourself, listen, write

Hallelujah! Amen. It is Done.

April 6

I Am...I Restrained

Almighty God, You are...
the Great I AM,
the First and Last,
All-Powerful,
Our Victor,
and the Winner!
A long time ago, at Calvary, You restrained evil, and You continue to do so.
You hold down, and push back the schemes of the devil.
Your Power is greater than any other power in the world.
Jesus, Your Name alone defeats the enemy.

God said to Moses, "*I AM WHO I AM.*" (Exodus 3:14)

Enjoy His presence: still yourself, listen, write

Provider

Father, we praise You for being our Provider.
We may not have what we want, but You do give us what we need.
You give riches that the world cannot give.
You give eternal life through Jesus Christ.
Jesus gives...
joy, even in the middle of trials and sufferings,
peace of mind, even when our circumstances haven't changed,
goodness, even when we don't deserve it,
and many more spiritual riches.
Help us to trust You more.
You know what we need.
Help us not to worry about money.
Help us to be better managers of Your money.
You own everything anyway.
You are in control even when things around us are falling apart.
Remind us each day that our Father is our Provider.

And my God will meet all your needs according to his glorious riches in Christ Jesus. (Phil. 4:19)

Enjoy His presence: still yourself, listen, write

Hallelujah! Amen. It is Done.

April 8

Party Tray

Holy Spirit, You are the Joy-Giver.

When there's trouble in our lives, You can give us a deep sense of well being.

You whisper in our hearts, "Everything is going to be okay," even when our situation has not changed.

Help us to look beyond our circumstances and trust in You.

You are Trustworthy.

Bring to our minds past and present blessings.

We have every reason to trust You.

Hold back discouragement.

Help us to refocus on the truth about our future.

Because of our faith in Jesus, and His resurrection power that lives within us...we know the best is yet to come.

Help us remember that You've planned a great party for those who believe.

May we live with the anticipation and joy that everything is going to be okay.

"Do not let your hearts be troubled. Trust in God; trust also in me. In my Father's house are many rooms; if it were not so, I would have told you. I am going there to prepare a place for you." (John 14:1-2)

Enjoy His presence: still yourself, listen, write

April 9

Empty Promises

Father, You are the One True God.
Thank You for giving Jesus to us.
Your Son is the image of You.
Your Holy Spirit brings precisely the truth.
Jesus is more than a prophet.
He is more than a good teacher.
Jesus came to testify to the truth; He is God.
There is One God...Father, Son, and Holy Spirit...connected and complete.
Create in us a hunger to know Your Word.
Jesus saves.
Jesus delivers.
Jesus heals.
Anyone else who claims to do so is a liar with empty promises.
Keep lies away from us.
Father, guard us from empty promises.

Even from your own number men will arise and distort the truth in order to draw away disciples after them. So be on your guard! (Acts 20:30-31)

Enjoy His presence: still yourself, listen, write

Hallelujah! Amen. It is Done.

April 10

Drawing

Holy Spirit of God, You are the Greatest Encourager.
You guide us and enable us to overcome.
You bring Light to the truth.
You are the Initiator.
Without Your urging and nudging, we would be lifeless.
You are the One who draws people to Jesus.
We, Your servants, cheer You on.
Draw us to the Truth!
Open minds and hearts to the truth about God's saving grace
through Jesus Christ. May people respond to You.
Draw them to Yourself.

**"No one can come to me unless the Father who sent me
draws him, and I will raise him up at the last day."** (John 6:44)

Enjoy His presence: still yourself, listen, write

April 11

Horizontal Hold

Praise and honor to You, Father, for Your Son Jesus.
He is our Rock.
He is our Stronghold.
No matter how high or how low our emotions go, Jesus is Steady and Secure.
In times of confusion help us to remember Your promises.
You don't break promises.
You are Faithful.
Your Word says You will never leave us.
You will stand by us no matter what.
Steady us Father, as we hold on to Jesus...our Hope.

Let us hold unswervingly to the hope we profess, for he who promised is faithful. (Heb. 10:23)

Enjoy His presence: still yourself, listen, write

Hallelujah! Amen. It is Done.

April 12

Ultimate Value

Father, You are Priceless.
We praise You for the Precious Blood of Jesus.
You are more precious than any gem or piece of gold.
You are the Best.
You are the Ultimate.
Help us to value Your Word that is worthy beyond any measure.
Open our minds and create in us an understanding of what is truly valuable in our lives.
Help us to cherish Your Word and never discount Your promises.
We praise You for the Power of Your Word.
Your Word cuts through anything.
Your Word is Truth, and that's what we desire to value.

The law from your mouth is more precious to me than thousands of pieces of silver and gold. (Psalm 119:72)

Enjoy His presence: still yourself, listen, write

Main Ingredient

Father, we may fill our lives with all kinds of things that take our time and energy, but Jesus is the Vital Ingredient.
He is the One who saves.
He is the One who gives peace in a troubled world.
He is our Hope.
Help us to hunger for the Truth.
Open wide our minds and hearts so we can feed on Your Living Word.
Your Word sustains us.
Your Word protects us.
Your Word feeds our hungry souls.
Help us to make Jesus the Main Ingredient in our lives.

For he satisfies the thirsty and fills the hungry with good things. (Psalm 107:9)

Enjoy His presence: still yourself, listen, write

Hallelujah! Amen. It is Done.

April 14

Our Hope

Father, Your Power is greater than any other power in the world.
Your transforming Power enables us to change.
You freely gave us Jesus as a Gift.
He was given to us so we could have life now, forever, and to the fullest.
When we turn from our sins and place our faith in Jesus, we are given His Power to overcome sin.
He can pull us up and out of dirty situations.
He can heal our broken emotions.
He can pull us up and out of those times when we're stuck in depression.
He gives strength and joy in the middle of...
troubles,
temptations,
and pain.
We can live a life of self-control and balance.
Jesus is our Hope.

For in the day of trouble he will keep me safe in his dwelling; he will hide me in the shelter of his tabernacle and set me high upon a rock. (Psalm 27:5)

Enjoy His presence: still yourself, listen, write

April 15

Table of Compromise

Loving Father, we praise You for Your Great Love.
Your Word clearly says that Your Love endures forever.
Thank You for loving us so much that You freely gave Your Only
Son Jesus, as atonement for our sins.
May we never choose to compromise the truth about Jesus.
He is the Only Way back to You.
His Word stands forever.
Give Your servants discernment so we can quickly recognize
and avoid any form of deceit.
Help us to leave situations when the truth is being twisted and
turned for selfish gain.
Strengthen us in Your Word.
Help us to stand strong and never approve a twist of the truth.
May the truth of Your Word never be diluted.

***The grass withers and the flowers fall, but the word of our
God stands forever.*** (Isaiah 40:8)

Enjoy His presence: still yourself, listen, write

Hallelujah! Amen. It is Done.

April 16

What Really Counts

Father, You Love us no matter...
if we win or lose,
if we're sad or happy,
if we're sick or healthy.
Your Love is unconditional and is not based on performance.
What You think about us is what really counts.
Help us to realize this everyday.
Push discouragement away from us when things don't go the way we had hoped.
Instead, remind us that we are Yours, and that's what really matters.
We lovingly kneel before You, because when it's all said and done, what You say really counts.

May your unfailing love be my comfort, according to your promise to your servant. (Psalm 119:76)

Enjoy His presence: still yourself, listen, write

April 17

Conviction

Father, You are a Holy God.
In order to come into Your presence we need Jesus.
He paid the price for our sins.
He died for each one of us, and He rose from the dead.
He's the Only One who has ever raised himself from the dead.
When we agree with You about our sins, and in faith accept Jesus as our Savior and Lord, His Holy Spirit comes to live within us.
Our bodies become temples of Your Holy Spirit.
We are not the same.
Our bodies take on new meaning.
We are made to be set apart and Christ-like.
Our physical bodies were not created to indulge in selfish desires.
Help those who have placed themselves in tempting sexual situations realize the magnitude of their actions.
Help them not to run from Your conviction.
Guilt is meant to help us turn away from sin and run to You.
Father, thank You, for giving us the Power to overcome temptation.
You are Gracious, and You want the very best for us.

When he comes, he will convict the world of guilt in regard to sin and righteousness and judgment. (John 16:8)

Enjoy His presence: still yourself, listen, write

Hallelujah! Amen. It is Done.

April 18

Growing in Jesus

Father, You give us everything we need.
You protect us.
You guide our steps.
You care for us.
You created believers to grow and be united in the Truth.
Create in us a desire to grow deeper with You.
Help us to grow healthy and strong in the Truth...the truth of Your Word.
Guide us step by step as we grow to maturity.
Open us up to Your teachings so we may have a deeper understanding of who we are, because of our faith in Jesus Christ.

Like newborn babies, crave spiritual milk, so that by it you may grow up in your salvation, now that you have tasted that the Lord is good. (1 Peter 2:2-3)

Enjoy His presence: still yourself, listen, write

Keep Your Head

Father, we praise You for Your Wisdom and Truth.
Thank You for doing just what You say You'll do.
Help us to always hold on to the truth of Your Word.
When pressure comes from people, steady us so we will not be shaken.
When we're under pressure, give us a clear mind.
Bring to our minds what You've taught us and shown us.
May we never compromise Your truth.
Help us to cling tight to Jesus no matter what our circumstances.
Remind us that You are in control.
Thank You for the calmness You bring.

They will turn their ears away from the truth and turn aside to myths. But you, keep your head in all situations, endure hardship, do the work of an evangelist, discharge all the duties of your ministry. (2 Tim. 4:4-5)

Enjoy His presence: still yourself, listen, write

Hallelujah! Amen. It is Done.

April 20

You Are Supreme

Father, You alone are God.
You are Supreme.
Jesus is the Only One who grants forgiveness and gives eternal
life.
He is the Gift of grace, and no one else.
Others have come and gone, but Jesus...
came,
died for us,
defeated death,
and arose from the dead on the third day.
He is Alive!
He is Real this day.
He is the Only One who is able to hold us together.
There is no one else like Jesus.

He is before all things, and in him all things hold together.
(Col. 1:17)

Enjoy His presence: still yourself, listen, write

April 21

Don't Worry

Father, You know what we need before we even ask.
You are in charge of everything.
You protect us day and night.
You are the Provider.
Help us to remember how You've taken care of us in the past.
Push back worry or anxiety concerning what we don't have.
Protect our minds from "what if" thoughts.
We choose to trust You.
You are God Most High.
We choose this day to place You first in our minds and hearts.
Thank You for guarding the way we think and feel.

But seek first his kingdom and his righteousness, and all these things will be given to you as well. Therefore do not worry about tomorrow, for tomorrow will worry about itself. Each day has enough trouble of its own. (Matt. 6:33-34)

Enjoy His presence: still yourself, listen, write

Hallelujah! Amen. It is Done.

April 22

Fresh Taste

Father, all good things come from You.
Thank You for giving us Jesus.
He is Your Gift of Grace.
Thank You for Your Goodness towards us when we don't deserve it.
You willingly want to give us a fresh taste of Your Goodness.
You want to pour out on us blessings of...
joy and peace,
love and patience,
and self-control.
Holy Spirit, help us to always seek a deeper relationship with Jesus.
Create in us a hunger to go deeper into Your Word.
Strengthen our prayer time.
Lord God, You are Good.
Help us to run to You.

Taste and see that the LORD is good; blessed is the man who takes refuge in him. (Psalm 34:8)

Enjoy His presence: still yourself, listen, write

The Keeper

Father, You are God.
You are so capable of keeping us through anything.
You can hold us together even when things are falling apart.
You can keep order and give security in chaotic circumstances.
We may be hurt, but Jesus can keep us from permanent harm.
Jesus is...
the Bridge that connects,
the Clip that holds us together,
and the Grip that holds us tight.
We are valuable to Him.
He keeps His eyes on us.
He keeps extending His Hand of mercy.
He keeps us in His care.
He keeps loving us....forevermore.

The LORD will keep you from all harm---he will watch over your life; the LORD will watch over your coming and going both now and forevermore. (Psalm 121:7-8)

Enjoy His presence: still yourself, listen, write

Hallelujah! Amen. It is Done.

Rise Above

Sovereign Father, You empower Your children.
Your Holy Spirit is the Power within us to rise above our circumstances.
Your presence is with us.
You give us the Power to overcome...
temptation,
fear,
worry,
addictions,
pain,
and obstacles throughout our lives.
Help us to trust You.
Jesus died a horrible death for us, death by crucifixion.
But on the third day He rose from the dead!
The tomb is empty!
He is alive!
Remind us daily that You enable us to rise above!
Thank You, Jesus, that You did...so we can.

The Sovereign LORD is my strength; he makes my feet like the feet of a deer, he enables me to go on the heights. (Hab. 3:19)

Enjoy His presence: still yourself, listen, write

April 25

Wake in Jesus

Jesus, You are the Light in our darkened world.
Your Holy Spirit is…
Real,
Honest,
and True.
You are alive and moving in the world.
Forgive us for becoming lazy and passive in our personal relationship with You.
By the Power of Your Holy Spirit, release in us anything that holds us back from actively pursuing a passionate relationship with Jesus.
Get us up and moving!
Help us to watch for You.
Awake in us a passion to actively follow Jesus.
Wake us up, O God!
Jesus is alive!

"He has risen! He is not here. See the place where they laid him." (Mark 16:6)

Enjoy His presence: still yourself, listen, write

Hallelujah! Amen. It is Done.

April 26

Your Testimony

Father, may Your Son, Jesus, be exalted forever.
He is Your Testimony.
He is the perfect representation of You.
He is exactly who You say He is.
He is the Lamb of God.
He is Savior.
He is King.
He is Lord.
We praise You for Your Word that testifies to the truth about Jesus.
May our testimonies of how Jesus changed our lives be evident to all.

We accept man's testimony, but God's testimony is greater because it is the testimony of God, which he has given about his Son. (1 John 5:9)

Enjoy His presence: still yourself, listen, write

Make New

Creator of All, You are worthy of our praise.
You took dust from the ground and formed us into Your image.
We bow to Your creative power.
You are Wonderful.
Holy Spirit of God, shape and mold our lives into Your design and purpose.
Open our closed minds and soften our hard hearts.
Give us a new start that only You can give.
Create in us a passion for Your Word.
Your Word changes minds and attitudes.
Your Word is powerful and true and can make us new.

Do not conform any longer to the pattern of this world, but be transformed by the renewing of your mind. Then you will be able to test and approve what God's will is---his good, pleasing and perfect will. (Rom. 12:2)

Enjoy His presence: still yourself, listen, write

Hallelujah! Amen. It is Done.

April 28

Velocity

Father, You are Powerful and in control.
We bow to Your plan that is already in motion.
Father God, we want to be part of Your movement.
We want Your will and Your perfect timing.
Holy Spirit of God, release Your Power and come quickly to bring...
salvation for the lost,
deliverance from evil,
peace to the sick,
and healing for our land.
Glorify Yourself, O God.
Come Holy Spirit, come!

Yet I am poor and needy; come quickly to me, O God.
You are my help and my deliverer; O LORD, do not delay.
(Psalm 70:5)

Enjoy His presence: still yourself, listen, write

April 29

In the Garden

Jesus, thank You for staying in the garden.
You didn't run out of the Garden of Gethsemane.
You stayed for us and was obedient to the Father's will.
Thank You, Jesus, for dying on the cross for our sins.
In honesty may we acknowledge before You any unconfessed sin in our lives.
Help us to stop making excuses and agree with You about the areas of our life that need to be more like You.
Pull us up and away from those things that are not pleasing to You.
You can remove our personal obstacles to Your grace.
Give us a contrite heart.
We want to grow deeper in love with You.

Create in me a pure heart, O God, and renew a steadfast spirit within me. (Psalm 51:10)

Enjoy His presence: still yourself, listen, write

Hallelujah! Amen. It is Done.

April 30

Fire Contained

Our Father, You are Holy and cannot stand sin.
Thank You for giving us Jesus who died for the forgiveness of our sins.
We believe that He is exactly who You say He is.
He is Savior and Lord.
His Holy Spirit lives within us...
protecting,
guiding,
teaching,
and correcting.
He is the Power that holds us and steadies us.
We want the Peace and Light of Jesus within us to burn brightly for others to see.
Holy Spirit, You are the fire contained within us.
Your presence is with us.

Again Jesus said, "Peace be with you! As the Father has sent me, I am sending you." And with that he breathed on them and said, "Receive the Holy Spirit." (John 20:21-22)

Enjoy His presence: still yourself, listen, write

May

Photo by Jennifer Taylor

Praise Him...*Hallelujah!*
Surrender to His will...*Amen.*
Live in faith as His plan unfolds...*It is done.*

Smooth

Our Father, we praise You for Your Son Jesus.
He makes everything okay even when it doesn't feel like it.
No matter what our past has been, or what we're going through now,
Jesus is able to smooth the rough spots out in our...
marriages,
families,
and jobs.
Lord, we have many questions to ask.
But for now, help us to stand on the truth of Your Word.
Your ways and thoughts are higher than ours.
Open our hearts to listen to Your Word and then obey.
Help us with the discipline of prayer and Bible study.
Jesus is our Only Hope in a rough world.
In Him...the best is yet to come.

Every valley shall be filled in, every mountain and hill made low. The crooked roads shall become straight, the rough ways smooth. (Luke 3:5)

Enjoy His presence: still yourself, listen, write

Hallelujah! Amen. It is Done.

May 2

King Rendered

O God, we praise You for Jesus.
He is the Way to deliverance.
He rendered His life for us.
We want to yield to King Jesus.
His will and way are best.
His timing is best.
Like Jesus, we want to have surrendered hearts and minds.
We thirst for King Jesus.
Help us to focus on the King.
Help us to surrender each day to His will and direction.
We want to be known as people who love Him deeply.
Anoint us with the oil of joy.
Your presence makes us glad.
We want to worship You forever.
We long to see You face to face.
We love You...King Jesus.

For you make me glad by your deeds, O LORD; I sing for joy at the works of your hands. (Psalm 92:4)

Enjoy His presence: still yourself, listen, write

May 3

Strong Right Arm

Father God, You are not weak.
You are Strong.
Nothing is impossible for You.
Our human strength is nothing in comparison to Your Power.
You can hold and carry our heaviest burdens.
You can pick us up and put us back together again.
You can change the toughest mind and soothe the deepest hurt.
Even when we don't feel You, the truth doesn't change.
You are near.
Nothing is stronger or greater than You...our LORD Jesus.

The LORD answered Moses, "Is the LORD's arm too short?"
(Numbers 11:23)

Enjoy His presence: still yourself, listen, write

Hallelujah! Amen. It is Done.

May 4

The Towel

Jesus, it was very moving when You washed the disciples' feet. You, Lord God, humbled Yourself and washed stinking, dirty feet.

You did this because of Your great Love for us and to teach us how to humbly serve others.

We want to be humble servants, but that can only happen with Your help.

Only Your Power, which lives within us, can enable us to serve unlovable, difficult people.

Serving others like You did can penetrate the hardest heart and the most stubborn mind.

We want to imitate You.

Let Your Power fall on us, as we learn to humbly serve…in the Name of Jesus Christ.

So he got up from the meal, took off his outer clothing, and wrapped a towel around his waist. After that, he poured water into a basin and began to wash his disciples feet, drying them with the towel that was wrapped around him. (John 13:4-5)

Enjoy His presence: still yourself, listen, write

May 5

Darkened World

Jesus, You are the Light in our darkened world.
Thank You for Your Living Word that stands firm and last forever.
We praise You for giving us Your Word as we walk through dark times.
Help us to shine brightly for You.
The truth of Your Word guides us.
Open minds that are closed to the truth.
You are...
the Only One who gives life,
the Messiah,
the Deliverer,
and the Light in this world.

Your word is a lamp to my feet and a light for my path.
(Psalm 119:105)

Enjoy His presence: still yourself, listen, write

Hallelujah! Amen. It is Done.

May 6

Words

Father, we praise You for being the Living Word.
Your Word is alive today and can cut through any lie.
Your Word is the truth.
We praise You for being a speaking God who desires to communicate with us.
Your Word...
encourages,
comforts,
teaches,
corrects,
protects,
and saves.
Lord, Your Word says that we are like salt in the world.
Our words are supposed to build each other up and bring out the best in others. And our words are to be spoken in love.
Help us Holy Spirit to speak in a spirit of love and not harshly or with unkind motives.
Our words reveal what's really in our hearts.
May our words bring healing and strength, instead of hurts and damage.

For out of the overflow of the heart the mouth speaks.
(Matt. 12:34)

Enjoy His presence: still yourself, listen, write

May 7

Supported

Our Father, Your Love is forevermore.
Your children can never be separated from Your Love.
Your Love is steady and strong.
Your Love is patient and faithful.
Your Love...
forgives,
holds,
guides,
and supports us as we grow.
Father, You know how hard life can be.
We get scared and change is hard.
But Your unfailing Love supports us in many ways.
Thank You for Your Word that guides and supports us.
Thank You for Your support through prayer.
Thank You for Christian friends that support us and encourage us.
Your Love, O Lord, brings strength and peace.

When I said, "My foot is slipping," your love, O LORD, supported me. (Psalm 94:18)

Enjoy His presence: still yourself, listen, write

Hallelujah! Amen. It is Done.

May 8

All We Need

Our Father, our hope is in You.
You are Lord God, and that says it all.
You are Truth, and that means You cannot lie.
Your Word says that You will meet all our needs.
When we feel like we can't go one more step, You supply the strength to go on. When the money runs out, You still take care of us.
When we're scared, You give us the courage to face our biggest fear.
When weakness sets in and obstacles are big, Your Power enables us to overcome. Jesus is our Only Hope for...
today,
tomorrow,
and forever.

And my God will meet all your needs according to his glorious riches in Christ Jesus. To our God and Father be glory for ever and ever. Amen. (Phil. 4:19-20)

Enjoy His presence: still yourself, listen, write

May 9

Follow

Father, You are Light.
You are the Truth.
You are Real and Trustworthy.
You are God.
Thank You for allowing us to have a personal relationship with You.
You only ask that we agree with You about our sins, and believe what You say about Jesus.
He is Your One and Only Son.
He is the Atonement for our sins.
He is the Only Way back to You.
He is alive now.
Father, soften hearts and open minds so people will respond to You with simple faith, saying...
"Yes, I believe that Jesus is who You say He is.
I trust Him as my Savior and Lord.
He is My Light in this dark world.
God, help me daily, to submit to Your lead and follow You.
Fill me with the joy of having a growing, deep, personal relationship with You."

"Whoever follows me will never walk in darkness, but will have the light of life." (John 8:12)

Enjoy His presence: still yourself, listen, write

Hallelujah! Amen. It is Done.

Discipline

Lord God, You are Love.
We say may times that God is Love, but we cannot truly grasp the extent and dept of Your Love.
Your Love is…
Unfailing,
Never-ending,
and Extravagant.
You Love us so much that You sent Jesus, the God-man for us.
Those who repent of their sins, and believe in Him, become Your children and live forever in Your Love.
You Love us so much that You discipline us for our good.
Help us not to get mad at You when You discipline us.
Help us to remember Your great Love and submissively receive Your discipline.

My son, do not despise the LORD's discipline and do not resent his rebuke, because the LORD disciplines those he loves, as a father the son he delights in. (Prov. 3:11-12)

Enjoy His presence: still yourself, listen, write

The Past is Over

Father, You cannot lie or break a promise.
We can completely trust You.
You are Almighty.
You have defeated evil.
We praise You for Jesus, Your Only Son.
He paid in full the price for our sins.
He wants us to be with Him.
When we turn from our sins, and place our faith in Jesus, our past sins are forgiven and forgotten.
Jesus can help us not to dwell on the past wrongs people have done to us.
He can help us to keep moving through any negative thoughts.
He brings healing and hope.
He can erase the hurts of the past, and give us a new future.

"Forget the former things; do not dwell on the past. See, I am doing a new thing!" (Isaiah 43:18-19)

Enjoy His presence: still yourself, listen, write

Hallelujah! Amen. It is Done.

May 12

Keep Going

Holy Spirit, You are the Greatest Encourager.
You cheer us on and enable us to keep going.
Remind us often that You are working even when we don't see it.
Help us not to focus our thinking on things that don't matter.
We want to keep our eyes on the Prize...our Jesus.
Fill us up with joy and faithfulness.
Give us the strength and boldness to keep going for Jesus.

May our Lord Jesus Christ himself and God our Father, who loved us and by his grace gave us eternal encouragement and good hope, encourage your hearts and strengthen you in every good deed and word. (2 Thess. 2:16-17)

Enjoy His presence: still yourself, listen, write

Godly Conduct

Father, You have prepared a place for us that's so good we can't even imagine how good.
You've prepared surprises and rewards for us.
Everything here on earth will not last.
You, Holy God, are forever.
Help those who are suffering financial hardships remember that Jesus will take care of them.
Remind us that everything we have belongs to You.
Create in us a willingness to share our possessions with others.
Help us to give up things that we hold too close to our hearts.
May our actions show an awareness that Jesus is near and the best is yet to come.

You sympathized with those in prison and joyfully accepted the confiscation of your property, because you knew that you yourselves had better and lasting possessions. (Heb. 10:34)

Enjoy His presence: still yourself, listen, write

Hallelujah! Amen. It is Done.

May 14

Lord God

Father, You are Lord God.
Those that agree with You about their sin and place their faith in
Your Only Son Jesus have Your Power living within them.
Teach us about the Power of Jesus within us.
Your Spirit is able to unlock closed hearts and minds.
You bring change.
You transform lives.
Help us to truly realize that when we allow You to be Lord over
every area of our lives, there is freedom!
Lord God, we place under Your lordship our...
spouses,
children,
families,
jobs,
money,
fears,
health,
everything!
You are the Lord of Peace.
You are Lord of Lords.
You are King of Kings.
You are God Most High!

Finally, be strong in the Lord and in his mighty power. (Eph. 6:10)

Enjoy His presence: still yourself, listen, write

May 15

Your Power

Almighty God, You placed the stars in the sky.
You hold the moon in its place.
You set the boundaries for the water in the oceans.
You control the…
wind,
rain,
sunshine,
and seasons.
You are God, and we are not.
Forgive us, Father, when we think too highly of ourselves.
We are made of…
dust,
bones,
and flesh.
We are nothing apart from You.
Our strength comes from You.
All Powerful God, we exalt You!

The Almighty is beyond our reach and exalted in power.
(Job 37:23)

Enjoy His presence: still yourself, listen, write

Hallelujah! Amen. It is Done.

May 16

Walk

Father, You are the Light in the world.
You are Truth.
You're the one sure Way to walk through life.
We don't have to fear anything with You by our side.
Help us to turn to Your Word when we don't know the next step to take.
Turn us to Your Word for...
direction,
correction,
and comfort.
Your Word says we can know Your voice.
You walk with us, and You will never leave us.
Enable us to walk in obedience and do what Your Word says.
Obedience brings joy.
What a joy it is to walk with You.

Let us walk in the light of the LORD. (Isaiah 2:5)

Enjoy His presence: still yourself, listen, write

Stop and Think

Father, only You are completely reliable.
We can trust You.
You are God.
Forgive us when we don't act like You are God.
Forgive us for placing ourselves and others above You.
Forgive us for our busy lifestyle.
We hurry from one thing to another.
Help us to stop each day and think of You.
Help us to get our priorities in order.
You alone are God.
You alone are completely trustworthy.
You alone are in control.
You alone are...
Redeemer,
Provider,
Powerful,
and Miracle Worker!

"Listen to this, Job; stop and consider God's wonders."
(Job 37:14)

Enjoy His presence: still yourself, listen, write

Hallelujah! Amen. It is Done.

May 18

Extended Love

Father, thank You for always reaching out to us.
Your arms are constantly open and extended to us.
Your Love is…
Everlasting,
Selfless,
Pursuing,
and Zealous.
Jesus' arms were extended in Love on the cross as He died for us.
Still today, His arms are extended in Love saying…
"Come, receive my free Gift of grace."
"My arms are around you and underneath you."
Father, take away whatever it is that keeps us from reaching out to You and growing deeper in love with You.
Teach us to let You love us according to Your plan.

The eternal God is your refuge, and underneath are the everlasting arms. (Deu. 33:27)

Enjoy His presence: still yourself, listen, write

Asked

Jesus, thank You for praying for us day and night.
Praise to You, Lord Jesus that You've already asked for us to be with You.
Thank You, Jesus, for asking that all believers be united as one, in You.
We can also rest in knowing that You've already asked that we be protected from the evil one and all his schemes.
What an awesome God You are.
Praise to Jesus, our Great Intercessor!
We rejoice knowing that...
You prayed,
are praying,
and will continue to pray for us.

In the same way, the Spirit helps us in our weakness. We do not know what we ought to pray for, but the Spirit himself intercedes for us with groans that words cannot express. And he who searches our hearts knows the mind of the Spirit, because the Spirit intercedes for the saints in accordance with God's will. (Rom. 8:26-27)

Enjoy His presence: still yourself, listen, write

Hallelujah! Amen. It is Done.

May 20

Things

Father, You own everything.
You are the Creator of Your universe.
You made us and placed us here to glorify You.
All glory belongs to You because You are God.
Forgive us for worshiping other things.
The things of this world can easily distract us from what's important.
Help us to throw to You all those things that distract us and keep us from a deeper relationship with Jesus.
Create in us a desire to make Jesus the top priority in our lives.
He is Lord God.

The earth is the LORD'S, and everything in it, the world, and all who live in it. (Psalm 24:1)

Enjoy His presence: still yourself, listen, write

May 21

Survivors

Jesus, because of our faith in You we are survivors.
Your grace frees us from the wages of sin, which is death.
Eternal life is given when we repent of our sins, and place our
faith in You.
Jesus doesn't promise that our lives will be trouble free.
But He does promise that He will never leave us, and He will pull
us through any circumstance.
He is...
the Pain Reliever,
the Joy Giver,
the Transformer,
the Prince of Peace,
and the One who can save our lives.
Holy Spirit, help people accept Your free Gift of grace.
Jesus is the Only One who makes us truly survivors.

Salvation is found in no one else, for there is no other name
under heaven given to men by which we must be saved.
(Acts 4:12)

Enjoy His presence: still yourself, listen, write

Hallelujah! Amen. It is Done.

May 22

Details

Father, show us Your Way.
We want to follow You.
Open our hearts and minds so we may see Your direction.
Help us to be obedient and trust Your direction.
We praise You for being a God of details.
Nothing is insignificant to You.
Every part of our life matters to You.
Father, help us to be patient.
We choose to trust Your timing as we wait for You to work out details.
We desire to remain faithful and committed to You.
Thank You for protecting and ordering the footsteps of Your people.
You are Good to us.

Show me your ways, O LORD, teach me your paths; guide me in your truth and teach me, for you are God my Savior, and my hope is in you all day long. (Psalm 25:4-5)

Enjoy His presence: still yourself, listen, write

God's Recipe

Father, You are Gracious.
You give us more than enough.
Thank You for giving us Jesus.
He is More Than Enough.
Open minds to Your gracious plan of salvation for us.
You freely gave Your One and Only Son as the Way back to You.
Jesus is God's Recipe for salvation.
When we follow God's Recipe, He mixes the ingredients of His Spirit into our lives.
He desires that we have an abundant life.

But the fruit of the Spirit is love, joy, peace, patience, kindness, goodness, faithfulness, gentleness and self-control. (Gal. 5:22-23)

Enjoy His presence: still yourself, listen, write

Hallelujah! Amen. It is Done.

May 24

Pushing Down

Father, You are in control no matter how out of control things get.
We praise You for Your Protection.
You are always interceding for us.
We are completely secure in Jesus, nothing can snatch us out of His Hand.
We can overcome because of His Power within us.
Thank You for pushing evil down.
We praise You for continuing to knock the enemy back for us.
Let us call on the Name of Jesus for help.
His Name encompasses who He is.
He is the One who forgives.
He is Powerful.
He is Our Deliverer.
He is Compassionate.
He Heals wounded minds and hearts.
He is the Messiah.
He alone saves!

Therefore God exalted him to the highest place and gave him the name that is above every name, that at the name of Jesus every knee should bow, in heaven and on earth and under the earth, and every tongue confess that Jesus Christ is Lord, to the glory of God the Father. (Phil. 2:9-11)

Enjoy His presence: still yourself, listen, write

May 25

Holy

Holy is the Name of Jesus.
Holy is the Lord.
Praise and honor to the Holy Spirit of God.
Father, we want to be more like Jesus.
We want more of Him and less of us.
May He increase and we decrease.
Help us to be strong when we are tempted.
Guard our minds, so we don't give into temptations.
Holy Spirit, help us to be obedient and self-controlled.
Thank You that You enable us to be what You've called us to be.
Remind us that we are set apart for You.
Thank You for Your sanctifying grace.

But just as he who called you is holy, so be holy in all you do; for it is written: "Be holy, because I am holy." (1 Peter 1:15-16)

Enjoy His presence: still yourself, listen, write

Hallelujah! Amen. It is Done.

May 26

Mark of Jesus

Gracious God, thank You for sending Jesus to save us.
Thank You for Your Gift of Grace.
Thank You for the Power and Protection of Your Son.
Remind us that because of our repentance and faith in Jesus...
our Savior and Lord, no other power has authority over us!
We are God's children.
The Holy Spirit of God has marked us with His presence.
We are free no matter what trouble we walk through.
With thanksgiving and praise, we take the mark of Jesus.

And you also were included in Christ when you heard the word of truth, the gospel of your salvation. Having believed, you were marked in him with a seal, the promised Holy Spirit. (Eph. 1:13)

Enjoy His presence: still yourself, listen, write

Guards the Course

Father, You have our best interests in mind.
You have a plan and a purpose for us.
The Christian life is not a sprint, instead it's like a long-distance run.
Each one of us has a special course You've marked out for us.
Your boundary of protection is guarding our course.
We thank You for the times You've protected us from intended harm and we didn't even know it.
Because of our repentance and faith in Jesus, we are winners and protected.
Joy and peace comes in knowing the One who guards our course.

He holds victory in store for the upright, he is a shield to those whose walk is blameless, for he guards the course of the just and protects the way of his faithful ones. (Prov. 2:7-8)

Enjoy His presence: still yourself, listen, write

Hallelujah! Amen. It is Done.

May 28

Sovereign Lord

Lord God, You are Almighty.
You are in control.
You are Number One.
You are King of the Kingdom.
Lord Jesus, in Your Name we ask that You release people from anxiety and depression.
Free us from anything pressing us down.
You can remove obstacles in our lives that want to steal our joy.
Give us the wisdom to learn how to get around those things that try to block us from peace.
Jesus has the answers.

But you are a shield around me, O LORD; you bestow glory on me and lift up my head. (Psalm 3:3)

Enjoy His presence: still yourself, listen, write

The Right Friends

Father, You call us friends.
Your presence is what we long for.
You love us.
You know how difficult this life can be with all the pulls and temptations of this world.
Give us Your supernatural ability to sense any harmful schemes of the enemy.
Empower us to sense danger and to use good judgment.
Keep us away from "friends" who pull us away from You.
Help us to choose our friends wisely.
Draw us to people who love You deeply, and are growing strong in their faith.
We need Your wisdom.
You are Wise.
You are Honest.
You are Loyal.
You are…Our Best Friend.

He who walks with the wise grows wise, but a companion of fools suffers harm. (Prov. 13:20)

Enjoy His presence: still yourself, listen, write

Hallelujah! Amen. It is Done.

May 30

Power Ride

Father, You are God.
You are Almighty.
Forgive us for not acting like You are Powerful.
Forgive us for quickly forgetting that You...
spoke things into existence,
stopped a raging storm,
and raised Yourself from the dead.
You can take care of anything.
No problem we have is out of Your reach.
You can take away hurtful memories.
You can defuse anger.
You can change our hearts.
You can change our minds.
You can fix things.
Your transforming Power is real.
Father, remove those things in our lives that are not good for us.
When things get tough, bring to our minds what You've taught us, and what You've done for us in the past.
Help us not to run back to old ways.
Instead, help us to run to Jesus.

"Ah, Sovereign LORD, you have made the heavens and the earth by your great power and outstretched arm. Nothing is too hard for you." (Jer. 32:17)

Enjoy His presence: still yourself, listen, write

Christ Our Lord

Father, thank You for giving us Jesus.
He is our Defender.
He is at Your right Hand praying for us.
He is our Mighty Warrior.
Thank You for always thinking about us.
Thank You for fighting for us.
We are blessed beyond words because of Your great Compassion for us.
The truth is, You are Christ our Lord and there is no one above You.
When we start to worry or feel jerked around in our minds, remind us to say Your Name.
The evil one shudders when he hears the Name of Jesus.
Strengthen us to choose to take captive every thought and make it obedient to Christ our Lord.
We need You...our Prince of Peace.

We demolish arguments and every pretension that sets itself up against the knowledge of God, and we take captive every thought to make it obedient to Christ.
(2 Cor. 10:5)

Enjoy His presence: still yourself, listen, write

Hallelujah! Amen. It is Done.

June

Photo by Cheryl Fairfield

Praise Him...*Hallelujah!*
Surrender to His will...*Amen.*
Live in faith as His plan unfolds...*It is done.*

June 1

Almighty Love

Father, You are the One True God.
Nothing can change that.
No matter how things look or what people say, You are Almighty God.
Your love for us is Zealous and Powerful.
Whatever big thing we come up against, it's never too big for You.
You stand ready to fight for us.
Your Almighty Love...
clears our way,
brings truth to our situation,
soothes past hurts,
forgives and forgets,
and pulls us through our greatest fear.
We bow to You and humbly say, "Thank You for loving us so much that You gave us Jesus."

For I am convinced that neither death nor life, neither angels nor demons, neither the present nor the future, nor any powers, neither height nor depth, nor anything else in all creation, will be able to separate us from the love of God that is in Christ Jesus our Lord. (Rom. 8:38-39)

Enjoy His presence: still yourself, listen, write

Hallelujah! Amen. It is Done.

June 2

Performance

Father, we humbly bow before You because You are God.
You are a Miracle-Working God.
We praise You and thank You for the times in our lives we knew
without a doubt that You had worked a miracle in our life.
Thank You for the miracle of ....
the birth of a baby,
a marriage restored,
a doctor's report that said "benign,"
a wayward child who comes home,
enough money to pay the bills,
and safety in an unsafe situation.
The evidence of Your presence goes on and on.
Even when things don't turn out like we had hoped, You are still
with us.
Looking back we see and remember Your Steadfast Love.
Looking forward, our hope is in Jesus.
Help us to remember that You look at our heart.
Performance is God's...we are made to worship Him.

***You are the God who performs miracles; you display your
power among the peoples***. (Psalm 77:14)

Enjoy His presence: still yourself, listen, write

God Is Love

Father, Your Love is...
Extravagant,
Unconditional,
Endures Forever,
Steadfast,
Trustworthy,
and True.
Teach us to love like You love.
Give us the will to love with commitment and obedience.
Help us to forgive each other.
Create in us a spirit of humility.
Enable us to unselfishly love others.
Set us apart and make us more like Jesus.
God is Love.

Love does not delight in evil but rejoices with the truth. It always protects, always trusts, always hopes, always perseveres. (1 Cor. 13:6-7)

Enjoy His presence: still yourself, listen, write

Hallelujah! Amen. It is Done.

June 4

Falsehood

Holy Spirit, there is nothing false about You.
You are the Truth.
Help us to quickly recognize a lie.
Ignite in us a desire to study Your Word.
Your Word is the truth.
We have to know the truth in order to recognize a lie.
Remove anything false, fake, or deceitful in Your Church.
We want to hear the Truth.
We want to speak the Truth.
Praise to Jesus who came to testify to the Truth.
Help us to be more like Him.

Therefore each of you must put off falsehood and speak truthfully to his neighbor, for we are all members of one body. (Eph. 4:25)

Enjoy His presence: still yourself, listen, write

June 5

The Drive

Holy Spirit, You are the fire that ignites us.
You create passion.
Create in us a drive to settle for nothing but the best.
Stir in us the passion to…
look for You,
know You,
and follow You to the finish.
Ignite in us an enthusiasm and a commitment to grow.
May we never be satisfied to just stay where we are, comfortable, with no growth.
Renew in us the desire to grow spiritually.
Remove spiritual laziness in us.
Help us, Father, to move to a deeper relationship with You.
Give us the drive to know You more.

When you send your Spirit, they are created, and you renew the face of the earth. (Psalm 104:30)

Enjoy His presence: still yourself, listen, write

Hallelujah! Amen. It is Done.

June 6

Learns

Holy Spirit, You are the Teacher.
Instill in us a teachable spirit and a love for learning.
Fill us up with Your Spirit...the Spirit of Truth.
You give understanding.
You give guidance.
You give discernment.
You give wisdom.
We are nourished and sustained by Your Word.
Create in us a desire to learn more and more about You.
Draw us near to You.

"It is written in the Prophets: 'They will all be taught by God.' Everyone who listens to the Father and learns from him comes to me." (John 6:45)

Enjoy His presence: still yourself, listen, write

June 7

Powerful Wind

Father God, we praise You for Your Power and Love.
We come to You as Your disciples.
Breathe into us a hunger to know more about who we are,
because of our faith in Jesus.
Your Spirit empowers us to overcome sin.
Teach us to lean on You.
Help us to trust You even more.
Your Power in us is greater than any other power in this world.
Because of You, we can have peace and joy in the middle of
painful circumstances. Holy Spirit, blow a fresh wind upon us.
Create in us a desire to know and follow Jesus.
Fill us up with Your Spirit.
Come, Holy Spirit, and revive us!

***Suddenly a sound like the blowing of a violent wind came
from heaven and filled the whole house where they were
sitting.*** (Acts 2:2)

Enjoy His presence: still yourself, listen, write

Hallelujah! Amen. It is Done.

June 8

Observer

Lord God, You have done great things.
We've seen evidence of You in many, many ways.
As watchmen we have seen You move.
Your plan is in motion.
We praise You that through prayer we are like observers of Your Word.
In Your time, You do what You say.
Open our eyes to Your Truth.
Show us and guide us in making decisions about our...
children,
aging parents,
jobs,
and money matters.
Make us observers of Jesus.
His life shows us the Way to go.

Show me your ways, O LORD, teach me your paths; guide me in your truth and teach me, for you are God my Savior, and my hope is in you all day long. (Psalm 25:4-5)

Enjoy His presence: still yourself, listen, write

The One

Glory to Him...the One true God!
Jesus is our Hope.
Nothing is too big for Jesus.
Praise and honor to the One whose Power cannot be contained.
His resurrection Power is ours, when we turn from our sins and place our faith in Him.
He's the One who overcame death, so we can live.
The transforming Power of His Holy Spirit can smooth out the rough places in our lives.
Jesus is the One who takes away hurts and confusion.
He brings joy and peace into our situations.
He can...
change minds,
fix our broken hearts,
and in His time, accomplish far more than what we could ever dream.
Help us to look to the One who gives hope.

May the God of hope fill you with all joy and peace as you trust in him, so that you may overflow with hope by the power of the Holy Spirit. (Rom. 15:13)

Enjoy His presence: still yourself, listen, write

Hallelujah! Amen. It is Done.

June 10

More Than Gold

Father, we thank You for Your Word.
Your Word is alive today.
Your Word became flesh and lived among us.
We praise Your Son, Jesus.
Your Word…
saves and delivers,
heals and comforts,
convicts and guides,
and steadies us in a shaky world.
What You say is far more valuable than gold.
Increase in us such a desire to seek You and Your promises.
Create in us a longing and curiosity for Your Word.
We praise You Father for giving us Your Living Word.

Because I love your commands more than gold, more than pure gold, and because I consider all your precepts right, I hate every wrong path. (Psalm 119:127-128)

Enjoy His presence: still yourself, listen, write

Dying to Self

Creator God, You hold us in the palm of Your Hand.
You are our Sustainer.
You are the Divine Potter.
You are All-Knowing, and All-Powerful.
Help us to always remember that we were formed and created by You.
We were nothing but dust until Your Hands touched us.
Holy Spirit, trim away selfishness in our hearts and minds.
Create in us a desire to have You as our focus and not ourselves.
Father, we invite Your Holy Spirit to breathe life into our being each day, empowering us to die to ourselves.
We desire what You want for our lives.
Master Potter...shape and mold us.

The LORD God formed the man from the dust of the ground and breathed into his nostrils the breath of life, and the man became a living being. (Gen. 2:7)

Enjoy His presence: still yourself, listen, write

Hallelujah! Amen. It is Done.

June 12

Seeds

Father, You make everything grow.
You are the Power that changes a seed into something new.
You are the Gardener.
Praise You, Father, for Your Way.
We desire that the seed of faith within us grow in rich ground with strong roots.
Protect us from the lies of the enemy.
The truth of Your Word is what deepens our roots.
Create in us a craving for the sweet taste of Your Word.
Turn us to Jesus.
He is the Light that produces growth.
Deepen our relationship with Him.
Grow our roots of faith…
deep,
steady,
and firmly planted.

But since he has no root, he lasts only a short time. When trouble or persecution comes because of the word, he quickly falls away. (Matt. 13:21)

Enjoy His presence: still yourself, listen, write

Faithful Witness

Thank You, Father, for sending Jesus…Your Faithful Witness.
He came to testify to the truth.
He testified that Your Love is unconditional and Your Power is transforming.
His life, death, resurrection, and ascension are testimonies of the truth of Your Word.
Father, send Your Spirit to pierce minds and hearts with Your truth.
May people not refuse to accept Your Faithful Witness.
Remove thoughts that would cause people to get entangled in deception.
Stop hearts from hardening to the point of refusing Your Gift of Grace.
Help us to be faithful witnesses of Jesus.

Grace and peace to you from him who is, and who was, and who is to come, and from the seven spirits before his throne, and from Jesus Christ, who is the faithful witness, the firstborn from the dead, and the ruler of the kings of the earth. (Rev. 1:4-5)

Enjoy His presence: still yourself, listen, write

Hallelujah! Amen. It is Done.

June 14

Jesus First

Father, we praise You for how You created the union of a man and a woman in marriage.
We praise You for marriage, and its order and design.
Your Almighty Power can break through any kind of barriers in a marriage.
No relationship is too dysfunctional for Jesus Christ.
Praise You for breakthroughs like...
forgiveness,
healing,
and the truth.
Holy Spirit move husbands and wives closer to Jesus.
May they cling to Jesus first and then to one another.
Strengthen them by the power of Your Word and the power of prayer.
May they stand firm in their commitment to love one another.
Help husbands and wives to look at each other through eyes of grace.
Thank You for fighting for marriages.
The battle is Yours and is fought by Your Power and Strength.
We praise You for Your movement in Christian marriages.

Finally, be strong in the Lord and in his mighty power. Put on the full armor of God so that you can take your stand against the devil's schemes. (Eph. 6:10-11)

Enjoy His presence: still yourself, listen, write

June 15

Readiness

Father, we praise You for true peace that is available in Jesus.
Prepare us and make us ready to tell people about the peace
that only Jesus can give.
Holy Spirit, enable us to have a readiness for sharing the gospel
with others.
Make us sensitive to Your leadings.
Help us to watch for those You bring to us.
Remind us that You make us ready even when we don't feel
like we're ready.
The Holy Spirit enables us to stand firm.
He gives us protective support as we share the truth about Jesus
with others.

***Stand firm then, with the belt of truth buckled around your
waist, with the breastplate of righteousness in place, and
with your feet fitted with the readiness that comes from the
gospel of peace***. (Eph. 6:14-15)

Enjoy His presence: still yourself, listen, write

Hallelujah! Amen. It is Done.

June 16

Mighty God

Father God, we praise You and thank You for Your Mighty strength and protection.
You are the Rock.
You are a Mighty Fortress.
You are the Wall that surrounds us.
Your dominion is Everlasting.
King Jesus will reign forever.
We praise You for delivering us and keeping us securely in Your Hand.
Jesus... we love You!

"Because he loves me," says the LORD, "I will rescue him; I will protect him, for he acknowledges my name." (Psalm 91:14)

Enjoy His presence: still yourself, listen, write

Trusting

Jesus...
King of Kings,
and Lord of Lords!
You are Trustworthy.
You are LORD God.
We choose to trust You.
May Your Name be exalted and glorified forever.
May we always trust in the Name of our Savior and Lord, Jesus Christ.
As we run the race that You've marked out for us, help us to keep our eyes on Him.
Help us to stay on course and grow into maturity.
Help us to run this race following You and trusting You, with all our hearts.

Some trust in chariots and some in horses, but we trust in the name of the LORD our God. (Psalm 20:7)

Enjoy His presence: still yourself, listen, write

Hallelujah! Amen. It is Done.

June 18

Living Water

Jesus is the Spring of Living Water that never runs dry.
His Living Water...
cleanses,
refreshes,
and restores our souls.
Jesus is the Only One who can save and satisfy our thirsty souls.
Forgive us for digging cisterns that hold dirty water.
Cisterns dug to hold our idols, such as...
money,
self,
and power.
Turn our nation away from any form of idolatry.
These cisterns of idolatry are cracked and can never last long,
and never completely satisfy.
May we recognize contaminated ways that twists the Truth.
The truth is that Jesus is the Spring of Living Water, now and forevermore.

My people have committed two sins: They have forsaken me, the spring of living water, and have dug their own cisterns, broken cisterns that cannot hold water. (Jer. 2:13)

Enjoy His presence: still yourself, listen, write

June 19

Treasure

Jesus...You are the Precious Treasure.
You are Priceless.
Your value is Unlimited.
You're the Only One who...
saves,
heals,
delivers,
and restores.
You are the Key to an abundant life.
Praise You for Your treasured wisdom found in Your Word.
Thank You for Your Love and Encouragement, as we search and accumulate the treasures of truth in Your Word.
Give us wisdom so we will recognize Your will.
Keep us strong as we search for understanding and wisdom, as we earnestly seek all the treasures found in Christ Jesus.

My purpose is that they may be encouraged in heart and united in love, so that they may have the full riches of complete understanding, in order that they may know the mystery of God, namely, Christ, in whom are hidden all the treasures of wisdom and knowledge. (Col. 2:2-3)

Enjoy His presence: still yourself, listen, write

Hallelujah! Amen. It is Done.

June 20

Your Heat

Father, thank You for never leaving us.
You are able to do whatever it takes to protect us.
You keep us.
Your Spirit is with us each day...
guiding,
encouraging,
strengthening,
and convicting us.
Sometimes You turn the heat up in our lives.
You use difficult times to build our endurance and strengthen our faith.
Make us strong and secure in You.
Enable us to stand against any type of external pressures that would try to weaken us.
Remind us when we're going through intense trials to keep our eyes on Jesus.
He holds us together when things are falling apart.
He cleanses us, soothes us, and makes us strong under pressure.

And he will stand, for the Lord is able to make him stand.
(Rom. 14:4)

Enjoy His presence: still yourself, listen, write

June 21

Your Banner

Praise to Jesus who is our Banner.
He covers us with His Love and Protection.
He stands in defense of His people.
And no power is a match for God.
Nothing can stand against Him.
His Power can destroy anything that would try to come against
His children.
Praise and honor to King Jesus...for He is God Almighty!

Moses built an altar and called it The LORD is my Banner.
(Ex. 17:15)

Enjoy His presence: still yourself, listen, write

Hallelujah! Amen. It is Done.

June 22

Saved by Faith

Father, You are Strong and Mighty to save.
You are Holy and will not tolerate sin.
Holy Spirit, help people admit they are sinners.
One sin is one too many before a Holy God.
Because of Your great Love for us, You gave us Jesus.
He is the Only Way back to You, Holy God.
He is our Redeemer.
He is our Rock.
He is the Truth.
Guard minds from deceitful twists that entangle the truth about Him.
Holy Spirit, help people place their faith in Jesus for salvation.
Our good works or moral lives cannot save us.
Jesus is the Only One who can save us from our sins.
He is the Lamb of God.
He is the Perfect Sacrifice.
He is the Only One who gives life, forevermore.
Jesus is God's Gift of Grace that we receive by faith...and are saved!

Jesus answered, "I am the way and the truth and the life. No one comes to the Father except through me." (John 14:6)

Enjoy His presence: still yourself, listen, write

June 23

Lift to Fix

Father, we want to lift up the Name of Jesus.
We want Him to be exalted because He is God, Most High.
Help us to get our eyes off ourselves and our circumstances.
Turn us from those established habits in our lives that turn us inward, instead of upward toward You.
Lift us up and draw us near to Jesus.
May we lift our hands in praise and surrender our hearts in worship.
Jesus is the Only One who can save us and permanently fix us.

"But I, when I am lifted up from the earth, will draw all men to myself." (John 12:32)

Enjoy His presence: still yourself, listen, write

Hallelujah! Amen. It is Done.

King

King Jesus, You are King of Kings and Lord of Lords.
You want to share Your kingdom with us!
What a Gracious King You are.
Holy Spirit, open hearts and minds to the truth about Jesus.
Forgive us of our sin of idolatry.
Forgive us of our arrogance and pride.
King Jesus is the Only One worthy of our worship.
No other king would do what King Jesus did.
Thank You for humbly washing dirty feet.
Thank You for dying for all of us, those who reject You, spit on You, and hurt You.
Thank You for praying for us.
Have mercy on us, King Jesus.
You are King and will reign forevermore!

The LORD is King for ever and ever. (Psalm 10:16)

Enjoy His presence: still yourself, listen, write

Steady

O God, praise and honor to You, Most High.
You are Steady, Secure, and Strong.
You are Ever-Present...
watching,
listening,
protecting,
guiding,
and teaching.
Your presence is real and evident.
You are all around us, even in the dark times of our lives.
Darkness is not even dark to You.
Thank You for Your Word that steadies us, and brings light into our situations.
We worship and adore You.
We praise You for Your Steadfast love that cannot be shaken.
Your Love endures for ever and ever.

We have this hope as an anchor for the soul, firm and secure. (Heb. 6:19)

Enjoy His presence: still yourself, listen, write

Hallelujah! Amen. It is Done.

June 26

The Judge

Praise and honor to You, Lord God.
You are the Judge.
Authority has been given to You to judge all people and all nations.
All will one day bow to You, Lord Jesus.
Lord God, You are the Only One worthy to be the Judge.
You are a Mighty Judge.
Forgive us for the sin of pride.
Teach us to humble ourselves before You.
Help us to serve others as You taught us how to serve.
You are the Good Shepherd.
We are Your sheep.
Empower us to humbly serve each other without being judgmental.
Forgive us for taking ourselves so seriously.
You are...Most High God.

Say among the nations, "The LORD reigns." The world is firmly established, it cannot be moved; he will judge the peoples with equity. (Psalm 96:10)

Enjoy His presence: still yourself, listen, write

Joined Together

Everlasting Father, each one of us is wonderfully made by You.
You created us uniquely different, yet belonging together.
No matter what country we live in,
or how we talk,
or what we look like,
we are united through Jesus.
Help us to see the beauty of diversity in Your Church.
Help us to love one another, and work together to glorify You.
Protect us, Father, from anything that would pull us apart.
Help us to lay aside ourselves and celebrate You...the Chief Cornerstone.

And in him you too are being built together to become a dwelling in which God lives by his Spirit. (Eph. 2:22)

Enjoy His presence: still yourself, listen, write

Hallelujah! Amen. It is Done.

Rich

Father, we praise You for Your Everlasting Love.
Thank You for our many blessings.
Jesus gives to us what this world cannot give.
He saves.
He delivers.
He restores.
He refreshes.
He can bring newness into long-time dead relationships.
We thank You for what You and You alone can do in marriages.
You are Compassionate.
You understand.
Nothing is too hard for You.
You are a Breakthrough God.
In Your time, You can make things better and better.
Fill us with the Power of Your Spirit.
Pour into marriages Your Spirit that enables couples to look at each other through the eyes of grace.
Your plan for husbands and wives is to be rich in love.
Have Your way in marriages today.

The LORD is gracious and compassionate, slow to anger and rich in love. The LORD is good to all; he has compassion on all he has made. (Psalm 145:8-9)

Enjoy His presence: still yourself, listen, write

June 29

King of Glory

Almighty Father, You are the King of Glory.
You are Strong and Mighty.
You are able to do more than what we could ever imagine or ask.
Holy Spirit of God, help us to turn each one of our battles over to You.
We can rest in the power and peace that comes from knowing that You are constantly praying for us.
Help us to realize daily that the battle is not ours, it's Yours.
No matter how things look, You are in control.
You can make something that appears to be so big and hopeless...small and foolish. You are the King of Glory.
No battle is too big for You.
Thank You, King Jesus, for fighting for us.

"This is what the LORD says to you: 'Do not be afraid or discouraged because of this vast army. For the battle is not yours, but God's.' " (2Chr. 20:15)

Enjoy His presence: still yourself, listen, write

Hallelujah! Amen. It is Done.

June 30

With God

Father, Your desire is for us to be with You.
Jesus submitted to Your will, so that through Him, we could live together with You.
Thank You, Father, for going all out for us.
You gave us Your One and Only Son.
You gave us Jesus to restore and save us.
When we come to Jesus and agree about our sins and place our faith in Him, we have eternal life with God.
No matter how hopeless or dirty a situation gets, He is always with us.
Thanks again for giving us Jesus, that Living Water that's with us...
soothing us,
giving us peace,
strengthening us when we feel we can't go on,
and providing safety from the enemy.
Nothing is too hard with You.

For nothing is impossible with God. (Luke 1:37)

Enjoy His presence: still yourself, listen, write

July

Photo by Cheryl Fairfield

Praise Him…*Hallelujah!*
Surrender to His will…*Amen.*
Live in faith as His plan unfolds…*It is done.*

July 1

Email: Pray All Day

Thank You, Father, that we have access to You any time, anywhere, all day.
Your children are connected to You.
We choose to join Your Holy Spirit and pray with You.
We often don't know what to pray, but You do.
We want what You want.
We lift our hearts to You.
Have Your way, Lord.
You are Sovereign.
You are Trustworthy.
Your protective Hand is covering and connecting us.
Thank You for praying for us all day.

For I am the LORD, your God, who takes hold of your right hand and says to you, Do not fear; I will help you. (Isaiah 41:13)

Enjoy His presence: still yourself, listen, write

Hallelujah! Amen. It is Done.

July 2

Not Just One Facet

You are the Great I AM.
We want to praise You because You are God.
You're like a precious diamond that has many facets that reflect Your Unlimited character and attributes.
Our minds cannot take in Your Greatness.
You are Powerful.
You are Faithful.
You are the Truth.
You are More Than Enough, and forevermore!
Help us never to put You in a box.
You are Supernatural.
Remind us that nothing is impossible for You.
You are God.

"Be still, and know that I am God; I will be exalted among the nations, I will be exalted in the earth." (Psalm 46:10)

Enjoy His presence: still yourself, listen, write

Pick This Day

Our Father, thank You so much for sending Jesus to save us.
He is the Perfect Sacrifice for our sins, Your Lamb.
Help people to accept Your precious Gift of Grace and not reject Him.
The Gift of eternal life is offered to all through Jesus Christ.
Help us, Father, not to brush off or brush away this good news.
Holy Spirit, open minds and hearts to believe the truth about Jesus.
He is exactly who He said He is...
the Messiah,
the One and Only,
the Lamb of God,
and King.
May people accept this day Jesus as their Savior and Lord.

I tell you, now is the time of God's favor, now is the day of salvation. (2Cor. 6:2)

Enjoy His presence: still yourself, listen, write

Hallelujah! Amen. It is Done.

July 4

Repent

Merciful Father, we praise You for Your grace.
We cry out asking for You to have mercy on our nation.
Forgive us for the sin of idolatry.
Help us to turn back to Jesus, our First Love.
Refocus us on Your Truth.
Your Word is the Truth.
Jesus came into the world to testify to the truth.
He is the Light of the world.
Holy Spirit, You are the Lampstand for our nation.
With joined voices, we cry out in repentance.
We ask that You revive our nation.
May Your Lampstand shine brightly throughout our nation...we pray.

Yet I hold this against you: You have forsaken your first love. Remember the height from which you have fallen! Repent and do the things you did at first. If you do not repent, I will come to you and remove your lampstand from its place. (Rev. 2:4-5)

Enjoy His presence: still yourself, listen, write

Freeing

Holy Spirit, You are Truth.
Your Word is true and freeing.
Your Word...
deliverers,
heals,
guides,
and saves.
Guard our thinking.
Protect us from false teachings that twist the truth.
Take away obstacles that confuse us and get us mixed up.
We want Your truth, because we know You cannot lie.
Applying the truth of Your Word in our lives brings change.
Your truth can free us from...
doubts,
lies,
and hurts.
Thank You for Jesus, our Gift of Grace.
He is True.
He is Right.
He is Compassionate.
He is Trustworthy.
Help us to be more and more like Him.
Thank You for the joy that comes in the presence of the Living
Word, which sets us free!

Then you will know the truth, and the truth will set you free.
(John 8:32)

Enjoy His presence: still yourself, listen, write

Hallelujah! Amen. It is Done.

Scepter

Father God, You rule over heaven and earth.
All Authority comes from You.
You are God Most High.
Help us to submit to Jesus…Your One and Only Son.
He is Mighty.
He is Strong.
He is Above All.
Even though things in this world seem to be falling apart, everything is really coming together, according to Your Word.
Praise and glory to You for reigning above all the nations.
Help us to grow stronger and stronger in You.
We want to remain faithful and obedient to Your will.
Thank You for Your Power and Strength.
You reign with Supreme Authority.
You are Sovereign over all.

She gave birth to a son, a male child, who will rule all the nations with an iron scepter. And her child was snatched up to God and to his throne. (Rev. 12:5)

Enjoy His presence: still yourself, listen, write

July 7

Behold

We praise You, Father, that no sin is too big for You when we give it to Jesus.
Evidence of Your forgiveness is in Your Word.
For example...
the adulteress woman,
the thief on the cross,
the woman at the well,
and Peter, who denied Jesus three times.
You are a Holy God who cannot tolerate sin.
We praise You, Father, for giving us Your One and Only Son, Jesus.
He died for our sins so we can live with You forever.
Jesus is the Only One who can forgive our sins.
Because of our repentance and faith in Jesus, nothing can separate us from Your love.
Thank You, that through Jesus, mercy is fresh and new each day.
Holy Spirit, change minds and hearts.
Help people to sincerely respond to Jesus with childlike faith and simply say...
"Holy God, I am a sinner. I believe Jesus died for my sins. I believe He rose from the dead. He's alive now. I place my faith in Him alone. I want to follow Him all the days of my life."

The next day John saw Jesus coming toward him and said, "Look, the Lamb of God, who takes away the sin of the world!" (John 1:29)

Enjoy His presence: still yourself, listen, write

Hallelujah! Amen. It is Done.

July 8

Obedience

Father, You are Holy.
You are Faithful and True.
You are Trustworthy.
We want to follow You.
Help us to respond to Your Way with a spirit of brokenness.
Forgive us for trying to do things in our own strength.
Empty our hearts of self-will.
Help us to respond to You with humility and obedience.
Lord, we ask that we do the very thing You have called us to do.
Help us not to resist Your way.
Because when it's all said and done, whatever You've called us to do is what will really count.
Holy Spirit, create in us a humble and submissive heart...ready to obey.

But Samuel replied: "Does the LORD delight in burnt offerings and sacrifices as much as in obeying the voice of the LORD? To obey is better than sacrifice, and to heed is better than the fat of rams." (1 Sam. 15:22)

Enjoy His presence: still yourself, listen, write

The Head

Our Father, You are the Head, and we are the Body of Christ...
Your Church.
We are under Your direction.
We ask for Your Spirit to stir within us a deep desire to be connected to Your will and Your way.
We want to be joined in service with fellow believers, and held together by You.
You have created each one of us for a purpose.
Each one of us has been given a special gift in order to reflect Jesus to others.
We need each other.
Help us to serve others and build each other up.
Draw us together in love.
Enable us to be patient with one another.
Give us good communication skills.
Help us to become good listeners.
Strengthen the Body of Christ, as we submit to the direction of the Head.

Instead, speaking the truth in love, we will in all things grow up into him who is the Head, that is, Christ. From him the whole body, joined and held together by every supporting ligament, grows and builds itself up in love, as each part does its work. (Eph. 4:15-16)

Enjoy His presence: still yourself, listen, write

Hallelujah! Amen. It is Done.

July 10

Melancholy

Father, Your eyes never look away from us.
You are always watching us and thinking about us.
You experienced feelings, too, such as...
loneliness,
rejection,
anger,
grief,
and being misunderstood.
You understand our feelings.
Protect our feelings, O Lord.
Help us to remember that feelings come and go, but You always stay.
Thank You for always praying for us.
Help us, Lord, when our spirits are low, to look up to You.
We praise You for being...
our Stabilizer,
our Anchor,
and our Perfect Balance.

Jesus wept. (John 11:35)

Enjoy His presence: still yourself, listen, write

July 11

Body of Christ

Father, we praise You for Your Power, which is at work within us.
Your mighty movement is within Your Church Body.
We humbly say, thank You, Jesus, for praying for us.
Thank You for asking that we be one with You and joined together with fellow believers.
Praise to You, O Lord, for glimpses of Your prayers being answered.
We join You, Lord, and ask that You grow us to a corporate maturity.
Guide us to the truth.
Draw us closer to You, as You teach us about fervent prayer.
Father, we want to know You more.
Deepen and mature our understanding of You.
Help us to stand strong…together…with You.

That all of them may be one, Father, just as you are in me and I am in you. May they also be in us so that the world may believe that you have sent me. I have given them the glory that you gave me, that they may be one as we are one. (John 17:21-22)

Enjoy His presence: still yourself, listen, write

Hallelujah! Amen. It is Done.

July 12

Double Portion

Gracious Father, Your Love is extravagant.
You love to lavish on Your children blessings of peace and strength.
May our motives be pure as we ask You to fill us up with a double portion of Your Spirit.
We want to hear You clearly as You guide us in the days to come.
Open our hearts and help us to respond to You.
We want to work with You and accomplish more, for You.
Teach us and strengthen us with the truth of Your Word.
Your kingdom come.
Your will be done.

My flesh and my heart may fail, but God is the strength of my heart and my portion forever. (Psalm 73:26)

Enjoy His presence: still yourself, listen, write

July 13

Strong, Stronger

Lord God, whatever comes from Your mouth is powerful.
You speak the Truth.
Many times You said..."I tell you the truth."
Thank You for the promise that You're always with us.
You give us Your strength as You shape and mold us.
You can bring peace and harmony in the weakened areas of
our lives.
Help us to walk humbly, while singing a melody of praises for...
Your protection,
Your joy,
and Your strength.
Thank You for making us strong and stronger as we praise You.
We place our lives in the Hands of the Strongest.

***O my Strength, I sing praise to you; you, O God, are my
fortress, my loving God.*** (Psalm 59:17)

Enjoy His presence: still yourself, listen, write

Hallelujah! Amen. It is Done.

July 14

Serving Like Jesus

Holy God, we humbly come to Your feet wanting to hear You.
Holy Spirit, teach us to listen to Your Word.
We want to be fruitful and faithful servants.
As we serve others, help us to serve like Jesus did...
loving the unlovable,
willing to be interrupted,
listening even when tired,
and willing to give up our rights.
As we serve others, guard us from distractions of any kind from
the enemy.
Stop the lies that want to steal our joy as we serve others.
Keep our eyes on You.
Keep us moving toward You.
Make us healthy and strong servants.
Praise to Jesus, our Humble Servant.

**She had a sister called Mary, who sat at the Lord's feet
listening to what he said. But Martha was distracted by all
the preparations that had to be made.** (Luke 10:39-40)

Enjoy His presence: still yourself, listen, write

Flash the Light

Thank You, Jesus, for being the Light of the World...
Pure,
Right,
Real,
and True.
Father, explode the fire of Your Spirit in our minds and hearts.
Empower us to be Your Light in a darkened world.
Help us to live our lives in a way that points to Jesus.
He showed us how to live a life that shines His Light.
Help us each day to put in a good word for Jesus.
Thank You, Lord, that we can live in the Light of Your truth.

"Neither do people light a lamp and put it under a bowl. Instead they put it on its stand, and it gives light to everyone in the house. In the same way, let your light shine before men, that they may see your good deeds and praise your Father in heaven." (Matt. 5:15-16)

Enjoy His presence: still yourself, listen, write

Hallelujah! Amen. It is Done.

July 16

Stone Remover

Mighty God, You are the Stone Remover.
You can remove the stones of past hurts deeply embedded in hearts.
You can remove the stones of lies that harden our minds.
You can remove anger that turned into stones of bitterness.
Your Power is transforming.
You are God Most High.
Father, in the Name of Jesus, we ask that You remove stones of…
past hurts,
lies,
and anger that has hardened hearts and minds.
Release Your healing Power and bring forgiveness.
We need Your Spirit to wash over us.
Bring truth and peace to our relationships and circumstances.
Nothing is too hard for You.

And they asked each other, "Who will roll the stone away from the entrance of the tomb?" But when they looked up, they saw that the stone, which was very large, had been rolled away. (Mark 16:3-4)

Enjoy His presence: still yourself, listen, write

Grace

Father, You are so Good to us.
We sincerely say, thank You for giving us Jesus.
He is Your One and Only Son.
He is the Lamb of God who freely gave His life for us.
We pray that people accept Your Gift of grace through Jesus Christ.
Grace forgives.
Grace covers everything.
Grace is available today.
Grace is Your Goodness towards us.
Your Love for us is extravagant.
We are the apple of Your eye.
We are constantly in Your sight.
We are always on Your mind as You shape and mold our lives.
Praise to You, Father, for Your wonderful grace!

For it is by grace you have been saved, through faith--- and this not from yourselves, it is the gift of God---not by works, so that no one can boast. (Eph. 2:8-9)

Enjoy His presence: still yourself, listen, write

Hallelujah! Amen. It is Done.

July 18

All God's People

O God, You are Creator of All and Maker of heaven and earth.
You made each one of us according to Your plan and purpose.
You like diversity and uniqueness.
You formed and shaped each one of us.
Pour Your Spirit upon us and fill us up.
Give us the power and boldness to tell all people about Your saving grace through Jesus Christ.
You want no one to be lost.
We pray that all people bow before You and say...
"Yes, Jesus is the Messiah and Lamb of God."
"Yes, Jesus is alive. He is my Savior and Lord."
"Yes, I will follow Him all the days of my life."

That at the name of Jesus every knee should bow, in heaven and on earth and under the earth, and every tongue confess that Jesus Christ is Lord, to the glory of God the Father. (Phil. 2:10-11)

Enjoy His presence: still yourself, listen, write

The Name of Jesus

Father, You exalted the Name of Jesus.
His Name is a perfect representation of You.
His Name reflects Your character...
the Authority,
the Only One who saves,
the Healer,
and the Deliverer!
The Name of Jesus is powerful because it stands for everything about Him.
Therefore, we praise the Name of Jesus.
In Him and through Him all things are possible.
Thank You for hearing and answering prayers according to Your...
will,
plan,
and timing.
May the Name of Jesus be glorified!

I tell you the truth, anyone who has faith in me will do what I have been doing. He will do even greater things than these, because I am going to the Father. And I will do whatever you ask in my name, so that the Son may bring glory to the Father. You may ask me for anything in my name, and I will do it. (John 14:12-14)

Enjoy His presence: still yourself, listen, write

Hallelujah! Amen. It is Done.

Nails

Jesus Christ...
the Messiah,
and our Savior.
Let the nails that drew the Blood of Jesus remind us that His Blood declares us not guilty.
Only His Blood grants forgiveness and gives us the power to overcome sin.
Thank You, Jesus, for taking the pain of the nails for us.
Thank You for overcoming death.
Help us, Lord, to live our lives in joy.
You are the Winner.
Thank You that we are winners, too... through Jesus Christ!
Therefore, nothing at all can separate us from Your Love.

Having canceled the written code, with its regulations, that was against us and that stood opposed to us; he took it away, nailing it to the cross. And having disarmed the powers and authorities, he made a public spectacle of them, triumphing over them by the cross. (Col. 2:14-15)

Enjoy His presence: still yourself, listen, write

False Teachers Among Us

Father, we praise You for always being with us.
You are an Everlasting Father.
You are the Truth.
You are the Beginning and the End.
You are the Great Time Keeper.
You make everything beautiful in Your time.
Help us not to take advantage of Your great Patience towards us.
Help us to passionately respond to Your invitation to grow deeper.
May the truth about You stay fresh in our minds.
Help us not to drift from the truth of Your Word.
With Your Mighty Hand hold back the lies and false teachings that can cause us to weaken.
Each day as we grow older, keep us strong in the truth and growing deeper in love with You.
Guard us, Father, because false teachers are among us.

But there were also false prophets among the people, just as there will be false teachers among you. They will secretly introduce destructive heresies, even denying the sovereign Lord who bought them---bringing swift destruction on themselves. Many will follow their shameful ways and will bring the way of truth into disrepute. (2 Peter 2:1-2)

Enjoy His presence: still yourself, listen, write

Hallelujah! Amen. It is Done.

July 22

Right to Recline

Father, You are Holy.
It is right to praise You and worship You.
Thank You for Your Only Son, Jesus.
His Blood gives forgiveness and life.
Holy Spirit, help us to lay down
excuses,
pride,
fears,
and ourselves at the foot of the cross.
It is right to bow and recline at the foot of the cross and remember
what Jesus did for us.
For He is…
Good,
Right,
True,
and worthy of our praise!

Come, let us bow down in worship, let us kneel before the LORD our Maker. (Psalm 95:6)

Enjoy His presence: still yourself, listen, write

July 23

Feeling Empty

Father, You are More Than Enough.
Your Love is overflowing and extravagant.
You desire to fill us with hope and joy.
You can bring contentment.
Help us, Father, when we feel empty to turn to You.
You are the Only One that can fill the empty places in our lives.
You can...
satisfy our lonely hearts,
bring calmness when things are falling apart,
and give peace in times of discomfort.
Hold back distractions that want to draw us away from Jesus.
Draw us closer to Him.
Create in us a willingness to spend more time with Him.
Help us to respond to His Love and Strength.
As believers, remind us of Your resurrection Power that lives within us.
Thank You for Your Power that enables us to be content in all circumstances.

I know what it is to be in need, and I know what it is to have plenty. I have learned the secret of being content in any and every situation, whether well fed or hungry, whether living in plenty or in want. I can do everything through him who gives me strength. (Phil. 4:12-13)

Enjoy His presence: still yourself, listen, write

Thank you for allowing me to become angry so to cause me to cry out. Show me why you are allowing trouble in my life + teach me (which requires great change from where I am) to be content in all circumstances.

Hallelujah! Amen. It is Done.

Abundance

Lord God, You are an Abundant God.
Lord, we give to You our…
time,
abilities,
money,
and resources.
We ask You to multiply what we have, so we can better serve You.
We want You to look good through us.
No matter how difficult or big our situation is, remind us once again of Your Greatness and Power.
Father, increase our faith.
Help us to remember all the things You have done for us in the past.
May we live with the expectation of Your help, and rest in Your constant presence with us.
You can take who we are, and multiply what we have, to bring to others an abundance of Your grace.

Jesus then took the loaves, gave thanks, and distributed to those who were seated as much as they wanted. He did the same with the fish. When they had all had enough to eat, he said to his disciples, "Gather the pieces that are left over. Let nothing be wasted." So they gathered them and filled twelve baskets with the pieces of the five barley loaves left over by those who had eaten. (John 6:11-13)

Enjoy His presence: still yourself, listen, write

Through Christ

Father, thank You for the victorious life we can live through Jesus.
Help us to remember that our strength comes through Him.
Create in us the motivation to seek Jesus.
Give us wisdom to understand Your Word.
Strength comes when we know who we are, because of our faith in Jesus.
Help us not to try to muscle things in our own strength.
Holy Spirit, we ask that You break in us any lie that we're believing and don't even know it.
May Your truth be revealed.
Through You we can experience peace and joy in the middle of our pain and struggles.
Jesus is our Strength.

I can do everything through him who gives me strength.
(Phil. 4:13)

Enjoy His presence: still yourself, listen, write

Hallelujah! Amen. It is Done.

July 26

Feeble Hands

Father...
Your Hands are steady.
Your Hands guard us.
Your Hands guide us along the way.
Your Hands cannot be over powered.
We desire to serve You.
We need our serving hands to be strengthened.
Strengthen us through Your Word.
Enable us to change.
We can easily become weak in times of distraction and confusion.
Lead us to the truth of Your Word, which enables us to become stronger and stronger.
May we be grounded in the Word of God as our hands reach out to serve.
Strengthen us, we pray.

Strengthen the feeble hands, steady the knees that give way. (Isaiah 35:3)

Enjoy His presence: still yourself, listen, write

Processes

Father, something is going on in the hearts of people.
You are moving in a series of actions, all to draw people to a personal relationship with Jesus, or to deepen their relationship with Him.
Step by step, piece-by-piece, You can change minds.
God is in the changing business.
Jesus is our Hope.
He can make all things new.
He can restore marriages.
He can deliver us from addictions.
He can renew our broken hearts.
He cares.
Your timing is hard to understand.
Strengthen each one of us as we individually go through the processes of healing and wholeness.
Give us the peace that comes from knowing You're working on our behalf and have our best interests in mind.

Being confident of this, that he who began a good work in you will carry it on to completion until the day of Christ Jesus. (Phil. 1:6)

Enjoy His presence: still yourself, listen, write

Hallelujah! Amen. It is Done.

Judicial

Father, You have authority over all people.
You are God.
The government rests on Your shoulders.
Guide our leaders with the wisdom from Your Word.
We bring You the judicial branch of our government.
May the truth always be revealed to the judges.
Give judges discernment so they will make godly decisions based on the truth.
Open the minds and hearts of judges in our court system to the everlasting truth, that the Ultimate Judge is LORD God.

For the LORD is our judge, the LORD is our lawgiver, the LORD is our king; it is he who will save us. (Isaiah 33:22)

Enjoy His presence: still yourself, listen, write

July 29

Generations

Father, we praise You for being the Great I AM.
You are Faithful and True.
You are Powerful.
You are not just the Beginning.
You are also the End and everything in between.
Your presence has been, is now and will be forever.
Holy Spirit, let us not hesitate to tell our children and grandchildren about the truth of Your Word and Your blessings.
Give us the words to confidently proclaim Your truth, and how You've powerfully worked in our lives.
You are...
Provider,
Protector,
and Redeemer!
Let us proclaim Your truth from generation to generation.

Even when I am old and gray, do not forsake me, O God, till I declare your power to the next generation, your might to all who are to come. (Psalm 71:18)

Enjoy His presence: still yourself, listen, write

Hallelujah! Amen. It is Done.

July 30

All of Them

Father, we praise You for Your Great Love.
You loved us so much that You gave Jesus, for all of us.
All of us are valuable in Your eyes...
young,
old,
fast,
slow,
great,
or small.
Help each one of us to be powerful reflections of Your Love.
Unite us with a spirit of humility as we work together.
Help the Body of Christ to build each other up, and not tear
each other down with gossip.
Help us to see the importance of each person as we serve You.
May Jesus be exalted, and glorified through all of us.

***That all of them may be one, Father, just as you are in me
and I am in you. May they also be in us so that the world
may believe that you have sent me.*** (John 17:21)

Enjoy His presence: still yourself, listen, write

Corrections

Father, we praise You for Your Unconditional Love.
Your Love is beyond what our limited minds can understand.
Out of Your great Love, You created the family: husband, wife, and children.
You want children to honor and respect their parents.
And, You want parents to lovingly discipline their children.
Your Word gives...
wisdom,
strength,
and understanding to parents, as well as children.
Help children to be open to godly corrections given by their parents.
Help children not to rebel or run from corrections like "your actions can easily lead to adultery."
Push back the lies of this world and help us to be open to the Light of Your guiding corrections.

My son, keep your father's commands and do not forsake your mother's teaching. For these commands are a lamp, this teaching is a light, and the corrections of discipline are the way to life. (Prov. 6:20, 23)

Enjoy His presence: still yourself, listen, write

Hallelujah! Amen. It is Done.

August

Photo by Cheryl Fairfield

Praise Him...*Hallelujah!*
Surrender to His will...*Amen.*
Live in faith as His plan unfolds...*It is done.*

August 1

Above All

Father, You are God.
You are the One and Only.
You are the Spirit of the Lord.
You are Most High and we are nothing apart from You.
Forgive our nation and the world for the times we've turned our backs on You.
Forgive us, Father, for the sin of idolatry.
We place ourselves far too high.
Oftentimes we worship the things of this world and we're not even aware of it, like placing above You...
our spouse,
our children,
our friends,
our jobs,
and our money.
Help us to realize that nothing in this world can permanently save us, or satisfy us.
Only You can save and satisfy forever.
Have mercy on us and change our hearts.
Help us to see the Truth and respond to Your Love.
You are Above All.

"I am the LORD your God...You shall have no other gods before me." (Deu. 5:6-7)

Enjoy His presence: still yourself, listen, write

Hallelujah! Amen. It is Done.

August 2

Alive With Christ

Thank You, Jesus, for Your saving Love.
You gave Your life for us.
You overcame death for us.
You are the Perfect Lamb sacrificed for our sins.
May we never forget that on the third day the tomb was empty!
By repenting of our sins and placing our faith in You, Savior and Lord of our lives, we, too, can experience Your resurrection power.
That same resurrection power helps us overcome sin, and grow.
Your Power enables us to live life now, in joy, during troubled times.
You are alive and with us...now and forever!
We are alive with Christ!

But thanks be to God, who always leads us in triumphal procession in Christ and through us spreads everywhere the fragrance of the knowledge of him. For we are to God the aroma of Christ among those who are being saved and those who are perishing. (2 Cor. 2:14-15)

Enjoy His presence: still yourself, listen, write

August 3

Pepper

Father, the battle is Yours.
You are the Mighty Warrior.
You are Most High.
You are the Ruler of All.
The evil one is no match for You.
Help us to recognize quickly when the evil one tries to...
distract us,
irritate us,
or make us think something is bigger and worse than it really is.
The devil is like pepper in the wind compared to the Powerful Word of God.
Help us each day to put on the full armor of God and stand firm.
Help us to be alert, pray, and know that...
Jesus is our Covering,
our Shield,
our Fortress,
and our Resting Place.

Finally, be strong in the Lord and in his mighty power. Put on the full armor of God so that you can take your stand against the devil's schemes. (Eph. 6:10-11)

Enjoy His presence: still yourself, listen, write

Hallelujah! Amen. It is Done.

August 4

Change Our Minds

Father, Your Son Jesus is the best!
He is Your Gift of Grace to all.
You give so freely.
Free those who have been tricked into believing the lies of this world.
May those whose minds have been controlled by lies be filled with the truth of Your Word.
Change our minds and open our hearts, so we may accept the truth.
Open our minds to willingly accept Your corrections.
Your Holy Spirit brings truth.
Send someone to speak the truth about Jesus, the Truth that brings life and peace.
Help people accept and respond to the good news that Jesus alone gives true freedom.
Holy Spirit...change our minds.

The mind of sinful man is death, but the mind controlled by the Spirit is life and peace. (Rom. 8:6)

Enjoy His presence: still yourself, listen, write

August 5

Battlefield

Father, You are a Mighty Warrior.
You are Commander and Chief.
We praise You and thank You for...
Your Precious Son,
The Lamb of God,
King Jesus.
We stand firm knowing that Your Power is greater than any other power.
When we walk through battles of...
worry,
fear,
or trials of any kind, remind us that You are with us.
Oftentimes the battlefield is in our minds.
Help us to surrender the battle to You when...
worries,
fears,
or negative thoughts come into our minds.
Father, we choose to join You, as You take captive our thoughts, and make them obedient to Jesus, our Savior and Lord.

We demolish arguments and every pretension that sets itself up against the knowledge of God, and we take captive every thought to make it obedient to Christ. (2 Cor. 10:5)

Enjoy His presence: still yourself, listen, write

Hallelujah! Amen. It is Done.

August 6

The Well

Jesus, thank You for Your Redeeming Love.
You are our Hope.
You are the Well that never runs dry.
You're always inviting us to...
come and find peace,
come and be forgiven,
come and be refreshed,
come and be restored.
Slow us down, Jesus, and help us not to pass You by.
Turn our attention Your way.
We need the Living Water, for our thirsty souls.

On that last and greatest day of the Feast, Jesus stood and said in a loud voice, "If anyone is thirsty, let him come to me and drink." Whoever believes in me, as the Scripture has said, streams of living water will flow from within him." (John 7:37-38)

Enjoy His presence: still yourself, listen, write

August 7

Refresh Your People

Father, thank You for Jesus.
He is...
our Hope,
our Savior,
our Deliverer,
our Help,
our Guide.
Help us to remember that when we go through difficult times that You are holding our hand and walking with us.
Help those that live in oppressive situations to see Your Fingerprints in their lives.
Give them a keen sense of Your presence.
Remind them that You are near.
Bring scriptures to their minds that reassures them of Your great Love.
Refresh Your people with great joy as they follow Jesus, Our Lord.

Whoever believes in me, as the Scripture has said, streams of living water will flow from within him. (John 7:38)

Enjoy His presence: still yourself, listen, write

Hallelujah! Amen. It is Done.

August 8

Our God Moves

Father God, nothing is impossible for You.
You can take the biggest obstacle and move it.
You are a Mountain Mover.
You are a Miracle Worker.
You are in the changing business.
Your transforming Power moves...
hearts and minds,
wills and emotions,
plans and circumstances.
Nothing is too big for You.
Thank You for this holy privilege of praying with You.
We will continue to pray as we wait on Your move, Lord God.

For nothing is impossible with God. (Luke 1:37)

Enjoy His presence: still yourself, listen, write

August 9

Spiritual Milk

Father, Your Word is alive and powerful.
Your Word...
delivers,
saves,
protects,
and changes lives.
Your Word cuts through anything.
You are a Breakthrough God.
Holy Spirit, clear away anything that would stop us from studying Your Word and growing in You.
Take away blocks that the enemy uses to keep us from Your Word such as busyness, and thoughts like, "I just don't understand."
Create in us a craving to know You more.
May our relationship with Jesus grow deeper and deeper.

Therefore, rid yourselves of all malice and all deceit, hypocrisy, envy, and slander of every kind. Like newborn babies, crave pure spiritual milk, so that by it you may grow up in your salvation, now that you have tasted that the Lord is good. (1 Peter 2:1-3)

Enjoy His presence: still yourself, listen, write

Hallelujah! Amen. It is Done.

August 10

Compile Options

Father, thank You so much for Jesus who is the exact representation of You.

Thank You for loving us so much that You gave us Your One and Only Son.

You say that whoever repents of their sins, and believes in Jesus, will live forever.

We're so grateful that Jesus was obedient and submitted to death on a cross for our sins.

He is the Lamb of God.

There is no other way to You.

We can compile a list of all the different options that the world offers, but they are counterfeits.

Jesus is Above all.

You are the Great I AM.

You are the Light of the World.

You are the Resurrection and Life.

You are the Gate.

There is none like You.

Holy Spirit of God, help us to see the truth about Jesus.

Father, help us to throw away our compiled list of other options we think will take us back to You.

For You are calling us to choose and respond to Jesus...the One True God.

Jesus answered, "I am the way and the truth and the life. No one comes to the Father except through me." (John 14:6)

Enjoy His presence: still yourself, listen, write

Drifting

Father, You give us everything we need in Jesus Christ.
He can satisfy our hungry, thirsty souls.
Jesus is the Way.
You said He's the Only Way back to You.
Help us to realize that nothing can take the place of a close relationship with Jesus. Help us not to give into the temptation to drift away from reading Your Word and spending quiet time with You in prayer.
Give us discernment so we can quickly recognize when we start to drift away from You.
Have mercy on us.
Holy Spirit of God, draw us close to Jesus.
He is Faithful and True.
He is Lord God.

Let us draw near to God with a sincere heart in full assurance of faith, having our hearts sprinkled to cleanse us from a guilty conscience and having our bodies washed with pure water. Let us hold unswervingly to the hope we profess, for he who promised is faithful. (Heb. 10:22-23)

Enjoy His presence: still yourself, listen, write

Hallelujah! Amen. It is Done.

August 12

Together

Everlasting Father, You created the family...
father,
mother,
children,
grandparents and more!
The design of the family reflects Your Love.
You created families to be together.
Father, protect families from anything that would...
scatter,
separate,
or dishonor the way You created families.
Father God, protect the children, and bless them.
Place Your Hand of protection upon the minds and hearts of children.
Guard what they see and hear.
Hold back any form of mental illness.
Make them mentally and emotionally stable.
May they grow in the grace and knowledge of Jesus.
Encourage and sustain grandparents.
Enable them to reflect Your love to their children and grandchildren.
We ask in the Name of Jesus...hold families together.

He is before all things, and in him all things hold together.
(Col. 1:17)

Enjoy His presence: still yourself, listen, write

August 13

Keep Dancing

We love You, Lord.
Thank You for life itself.
We choose to keep dancing with You.
Help us to follow Your lead.
Help us to persevere and not grow weary.
Step by step, You will lead us through our struggles and circumstances.
Father, remind us that You have prepared a great place for us.
Our citizenship is in heaven.
May we bring others to this dance with You, because there's nothing better than having a personal relationship with Jesus.
For You, O God, are Most High.
Help us to keep dancing.
You are the Leader, and what You started in us You will complete.

Being confident of this, that he who began a good work in you will carry it on to completion until the day of Christ Jesus. (Phil. 1:6)

Enjoy His presence: still yourself, listen, write

Hallelujah! Amen. It is Done.

August 14

Just Married

O God, You are a Great God.
You created marriage and we praise You for Your design.
You are the Power and Covering that enables marriages to last.
You are the glue that holds husbands and wives together.
Help us to realize the union between man and woman is sacred.
We're not "just married."
Protect husbands and wives from anything that would try to separate them.
Create in husbands and wives a desire to place You first in their marriage.
Help them to seek Your guidance and then follow Your lead.

Trust in the LORD with all your heart and lean not on your own understanding; in all your ways acknowledge him, and he will make your paths straight. (Prov. 3:5-6)

Enjoy His presence: still yourself, listen, write

August 15

God Keeps His Promises

Father, when You say something You mean it.
You don't take back a promise.
You promised that You will never leave us.
You promised that You will walk through the fire with us.
You said You understand.
You said You will hold our right hand and pull us through.
Your grip is tight.
You won't let go.
During these hard times, remind us often throughout our days of
Your Steadfast promises.
Bring scriptures to our minds.
Help us to feel deeply the security You give us.
You are God.
You are Strong.
You are our Hope.
We can rest secure in what You say in Your Word.

*It is impossible for God to lie, we who have fled to take hold
of the hope offered to us may be greatly encouraged. We
have this hope as an anchor for the soul, firm and secure*.
(Heb. 6:18-19)

Enjoy His presence: still yourself, listen, write

Hallelujah! Amen. It is Done.

August 16

You Are Mine

Loving Father, we become Your children when we...
agree that we are sinners,
choose to turn from our sin,
place our faith in Jesus,
and commit to follow Him.
We then have a permanent position by Your side.
Your Love...
never changes,
is unconditional,
unlimited,
and everlasting.
When trouble comes, remind us of Your great Love.
When we go through tough times it's so easy to try to fight things in our own strength.
We want to rest in Your strength and allow You to help us through our difficult times.
Push back fear in our minds and bring forward a peace that only You can give.
You are our Help.
You are our Strength.
In good times and in bad times we are Yours.

"Fear not, for I have redeemed you; I have summoned you by name; you are mine. When you pass through the waters, I will be with you; and when you pass through the rivers, they will not sweep over you. When you walk through the fire, you will not be burned; the flames will not set you ablaze." (Isaiah 43:1-2)

Enjoy His presence: still yourself, listen, write

August 17

Remember

Father, we praise You for Your Faithfulness.
You know that when things get tough and we go through great suffering, we can easily forget how You've been there for us in the past.
Help us to remember the times in our lives when we said, "Only God could do that." When we feel like our situation is getting worse and our trial is too painful,
whisper again those words into our heart, "Never will I leave you."
Bring memories to our minds of how You've protected us.
Remind us again of how the money we needed came unexpectedly.
Bring to our attention of how You've changed our lives for the better.
Father, we choose to praise You, and remember Your Steadfast Love.

Remember the wonders he has done, his miracles, and the judgments he pronounced. (1 Chr. 16:12)

Enjoy His presence: still yourself, listen, write

Hallelujah! Amen. It is Done.

August 18

To See Clearly

Father, You see everything.
You are Gracious.
You are Compassionate.
You are also the Judge.
Help us, Holy Spirit, to see clearly Your truths and promises written in Your Word.
Remove in us anything that clouds our ability to see and know the truth about Jesus.
Lord, we need a keen sense of discernment, so we will see and know quickly what is true and what is a lie.
Give us Your Patience and Kindness when dealing with others.
Help us to speak to others in ways that are loving and honest.
Empower us with Your ability to look at others through eyes of grace.
Convict us with a willingness to examine our own lives too.
Help us to see the areas of our lives that need to be more like You, and less of us.
Enable us to see clearly the truth.

"Why do you look at the speck of sawdust in your brother's eye and pay no attention to the plank in your own eye? How can you say to your brother, 'Let me take the speck out of your eye,' when all the time there is a plank in your own eye? You hypocrite, first take the plank out of your own eye, and then you will see clearly to remove the speck from your brother's eye." (Matt. 7:3-5)

Enjoy His presence: still yourself, listen, write

This Place

Father, over and over, throughout Your Word, You have shown us that You do provide for us.
Help us remember...
the manna,
the ram,
the widow's bread,
the raven that fed Elijah,
the leper who was healed,
the strength of Gideon's army,
Noah's boat,
the courage of the martyrs,
and Jesus Christ the Messiah.
Your Power enables us to walk through difficult times, because You are with us.
Deepen our commitment to You.
Help us to trust You more.
Fill us through and through with an awareness of Your ability to provide for us.
We may not get everything we want, but You give us what we need.
Father, no matter what place we're in right now, increase our faith so we can confidently say..."My God will provide for me in this place."

Abraham looked up and there in a thicket he saw a ram caught by its horns. He went over and took the ram and sacrificed it as a burnt offering instead of his son. So Abraham called that place The LORD Will Provide. And to this day it is said, "On the mountain of the LORD it will be provided." (Gen. 22:13-14)

Enjoy His presence: still yourself, listen, write

Hallelujah! Amen. It is Done.

Dancer

Father, we choose to forever thank You for being Lord God.
We want to always follow Your lead.
Help us to lean into You and rest in Your ways.
As You turn us, we want to relax and smile, knowing You have a better way.
Hold on to us tight, Lord.
When we once again start to look at ourselves and other things around us, take Your Hand and turn our faces toward You.
Help us to lean into Your embrace.
Living a life following You is like dancing…step by step, in Your arms.
What joy to be part of Your movement.
Your kingdom come!

You turned my wailing into dancing; you removed my sackcloth and clothed me with joy, that my heart may sing to you and not be silent. O LORD my God, I will give you thanks forever. (Psalm 30:11-12)

Enjoy His presence: still yourself, listen, write

For All

Father, You are a Holy God who cannot tolerate sin.
We are eternally grateful for Jesus.
He is the Perfect Lamb who takes away all sins, for all people who come to Him.
No matter where you live, what language you speak, or what color your skin, God's grace is for all.
Help us not to take the death of Jesus lightly.
We cannot save ourselves.
We need Him.
He is our Savior.
Open minds and hearts so they will accept Your Gift of Jesus and live forever!

He sacrificed for their sins once for all when he offered himself. (Heb. 7:27)

Enjoy His presence: still yourself, listen, write

Hallelujah! Amen. It is Done.

August 22

Transformation

Father, You are the Master Potter, shaping and renewing us.
Your plan is to mold us, and transform us, making us more like Jesus.
He was obedient,
joyful,
and honored by You.
Help us to allow Your transforming Power to undo lies and redirect our minds to the truth of Your Word.
Create in us a passion to study Your Word.
Enlighten our minds so we can understand and apply Your Word in our lives.
Help us not to give up.
Help us to keep growing.
Open us to Your changes.
Refresh and renew our minds.
Make us more like Jesus.

Do not conform any longer to the pattern of this world, but be transformed by the renewing of your mind. (Rom. 12:2)

Enjoy His presence: still yourself, listen, write

August 23

Contrite Heart

Father God, You are the Potter.
We choose to be like clay in Your Hands.
Shape and mold us more like Jesus.
Help us to yield to Your Hands as You form us according to Your purpose.
We come broken before You.
We choose to give to You any part of us that needs to be restored and reshaped.
We want You to increase and for us to decrease.
We give our hearts, souls, and minds to You.
We want to rest in Your Hands because we know You will not harm us.
Your timing is the best for us.
We love You, Lord Jesus, our Savior.

The sacrifices of God are a broken spirit; a broken and contrite heart, O God, you will not despise. (Psalm 51:17)

Enjoy His presence: still yourself, listen, write

Hallelujah! Amen. It is Done.

August 24

Held and Carried

Father, You are God.
There is nothing, and no one above You.
Anything or anybody that tries to take Your place is a liar.
For there is only one True God, and His Name is Jesus.
He alone has the Power to save.
His arms are Powerful.
His hands are Strong.
He alone carries us and pulls us through places that are far too heavy for us to bear. He holds us tight and sustains us with His Mighty Love.
We are held and carried in His Loving arms...forevermore.

Even to your old age and gray hairs I am he, I am he who will sustain you. I have made you and I will carry you; I will sustain you and I will rescue you. (Isaiah 46:4)

Enjoy His presence: still yourself, listen, write

August 25

Entangles

Father God, thank You for Jesus.
He paid the price for our sins.
Through Him we are forgiven.
Holy Spirit, we ask that our hearts and minds be opened to Your corrections.
Help us accept Your conviction.
You are not the accuser.
You are the Master Potter.
Your sanctifying grace molds and shapes us.
Your Loving hands want to make us more and more like Jesus.
With Gracious hands, remove the sin that weighs us down.
Help us not to get tangled up in...
pride,
hurts,
bitterness,
and with the wrong friends.
You know what easily entangles our thoughts and emotions.
We want to be bright witnesses of You.

Heb. 12:1 Therefore, since we are surrounded by such a great cloud of witnesses, let us throw off everything that hinders and the sin that so easily entangles, and let us run with perseverance the race marked out for us. (Heb. 12:1)

Enjoy His presence: still yourself, listen, write

Hallelujah! Amen. It is Done.

August 26

The Key

Praise and more praises to You, Father, for providing the Way for us to come to You.

Jesus is the Way.

He is the Only Key that opens the door to eternal life.

Holy Spirit of God, draw people to You.

Stir up in them a desire to take the Key.

Today is the day of salvation.

These are days of grace.

Help those who do not have a personal relationship with Jesus to accept His grace. He freely offers grace.

He is the Key that unlocks the darkness of death and opens the door to new life.

He is the Key to life now and forevermore.

He will be the sure foundation for your times, a rich store of salvation and wisdom and knowledge; the fear of the LORD is the key to this treasure. (Isaiah 33:6)

Enjoy His presence: still yourself, listen, write

Fitted and Holy

Father God, You are Holy.
Thank You for Jesus, the Perfect Sacrifice for all.
His grace extends to all.
When we repent of our sins,
place our faith in Jesus,
and follow Him,
we are saved and protected.
Make our feet fitted with confidence and ready to share Your
gospel that brings peace.
Set us apart as Your servants...
holy,
ready,
and fitted with Your Mighty Power.
Help us to be our best for You.
For Your name's sake, make us holy.

*I am the LORD your God; consecrate yourselves and be
holy, because I am holy.* (Lev. 11:44)

Enjoy His presence: still yourself, listen, write

Hallelujah! Amen. It is Done.

August 28

Your Light

Jesus, You are the Light of the world.
You are the perfect representation of the Father.
We want to be reflections of You.
Help us realize that You created us in Your image.
May we not hide Your Light that lives within us.
As we become more like You and less of ourselves, we become
a bright reflection of Your Love and Power.
May each one of us do our part to make You look good.
Together we can be a brilliant representation of You.

**In the same way, let your light shine before men, that
they may see your good deeds and praise your Father in
heaven.** (Matt. 5:16)

Enjoy His presence: still yourself, listen, write

August 29

Keep Praying

Thank You, Jesus, for continuing to pray for us each and every day.
You never give up on us.
Thank You that You didn't run away from that horrible crucifixion.
You hung and died on a cross for each one of us.
You kept on going and followed through with the plan for our salvation.
Help us to be persevering people.
Your Power enables us to keep going even when we don't feel like it.
Help us to keep on praying even when we don't see our prayers being answered. May we keep on knocking in prayer, and in Your perfect timing, the door will be opened!
O God, thank You for hearing our prayers.

Ask and it will be given to you; seek and you will find; knock and the door will be opened to you. For everyone who asks receives; he who seeks finds; and to him who knocks, the door will be opened. (Matt. 7:7-8)

Enjoy His presence: still yourself, listen, write

Hallelujah! Amen. It is Done.

August 30

We're Cooking

Father, Your Power is transforming.
The most difficult, You can change.
You change hearts.
You change minds.
You…
restore,
soften,
and refresh.
When things get tough and we feel like we're going through a time of testing, help us to remember that we belong to You.
Your testing is a good thing.
You don't test us to see us fail.
Instead, You love us and want to prepare us and make us stronger for the days to come.
We want to walk this life out according to Your plan and purpose for us.
Make us useful vessels that displays Your glory.
As the heat is turned up in our lives and we feel like we're cooking, help us to be a fragrant offering to You.
Thank You for softening our hearts and making us stronger for You.

Yet, O LORD, you are our Father. We are the clay, you are the potter; we are all the work of your hand. (Isaiah 64:8)

Enjoy His presence: still yourself, listen, write

August 31

Your Face

O God, You are Sufficient.
You are the Maker of all things.
Your Spirit...
renews,
changes,
and empowers.
You can handle anything and anybody.
Pour out Your transforming Power.
Renew the face of the earth.
May Your Power change people from the inside out.
Help us to seek Your face.
Let Your glory fall.

Look to the LORD and his strength; seek his face always.
(Psalm 105:4)

Enjoy His presence: still yourself, listen, write

Hallelujah! Amen. It is Done.

September

Photo by Jennifer Taylor

Praise Him...*Hallelujah!*
Surrender to His will...*Amen.*
Live in faith as His plan unfolds...*It is done.*

September 1

Precious Root

Father, thank You for Jesus.
He is the Root.
He is the Root of Jesse.
He is the Root of David.
To this day, He is still despised and rejected by so many.
Forgive us for skipping over Him.
Help us not to pass Him by.
May people see His importance.
Open people's minds and hearts so they will accept the truth about Jesus' life and His work.
Strengthen Christians today so we can reflect the extraordinary nature of Jesus.
May we be rooted in God's Word and grow to know Him more and more.

He grew up before him like a tender shoot, and like a root out of dry ground. He had no beauty or majesty to attract us to him, nothing in his appearance that we should desire him. He was despised and rejected by men, a man of sorrows, and familiar with suffering. Like one from whom men hide their faces he was despised, and we esteemed him not. (Isaiah 53:2-3)

Enjoy His presence: still yourself, listen, write

Hallelujah! Amen. It is Done.

September 2

Of What Value Is an Idol?

Father, You are Maker and Creator.
There is no one like You.
You are the One True God.
You are Gracious.
Lord Jesus…
loves us,
saves us,
changes us,
cares for us,
and gives us hope.
Holy Spirit, help us to see the truth about Jesus.
Help us not to place anything or anybody above Him.
Father, forgive our nation and any person who in some way believes that something or somebody has more power than You.
You are the Only One who can restore us and satisfy us.
You are Lord God.

"I am the LORD; that is my name! I will not give my glory to another or my praise to idols." (Isaiah 42:8)

Enjoy His presence: still yourself, listen, write

September 3

Authentic

Father, You are more precious than silver or gold.
Your value cannot be measured because You are God.
Holy Spirit, help people to see the truth about Jesus and not be attracted to a fake.
Jesus is Genuine.
He is Real.
He does what He says He'll do.
You can count on Him for everything.
He is alive today.
We need to know Your Word so we can quickly discern what is authentic and what is fake.
Help us not to belong to anything that is not of You.
The truth is...Jesus is Authentic.

This is how you can recognize the Spirit of God: Every spirit that acknowledges that Jesus Christ has come in the flesh is from God, but every spirit that does not acknowledge Jesus is not from God. (1 John 4:2-3)

Enjoy His presence: still yourself, listen, write

Hallelujah! Amen. It is Done.

September 4

Rearranging and Changing

You, O God, are King.
You are triumphant over the earth and all people.
Your reign is forever.
Your Holy Spirit enables us to change.
Your Power is able to move obstacles in our lives.
You are God.
You push back the dirt in our lives in order to bring newness and growth.
You, O God, because of Your great Love, are constantly thinking and fighting for us.
You are in the business of...
saving us,
healing us,
changing us,
and delivering us.
Jesus rearranges and changes our lives for the better.

As Saul turned to leave Samuel, God changed Saul's heart, and all these signs were fulfilled that day. (1 Sam. 10:9)

Enjoy His presence: still yourself, listen, write

September 5

Tender and Together

O God, You are our Father.
We belong to Your family when we repent of our sins and place our faith in Jesus. That makes us Your children.
You desire that Your children get along with each other, and be together.
Remind us, Lord, that even though all of us are unfinished, each one of us is still special in Your eyes.
Help us to love one another with tenderness and compassion.
Your Tender Hands are still shaping and molding us.
You have a special purpose for each one of us.
You have a wonderful plan for us individually and together.
Help us to come together in Jesus' Name.

If you have any encouragement from being united with Christ, if any comfort from his love, if any fellowship with the Spirit, if any tenderness and compassion, then make my joy complete by being like-minded, having the same love, being one in spirit and purpose. (Phil. 2:1-2)

Enjoy His presence: still yourself, listen, write

Hallelujah! Amen. It is Done.

September 6

Our Future Glory

Father, we are excited and encouraged about our future glory.
The best is yet to come!
Someday there will be harmony and peace even in nature.
Creation itself longs for that day.
Until then, let us persevere and continue to bring the healing
presence of Jesus to a broken world.
May we always remember that we are people of great hope,
because our future is secure in Jesus.
Strengthen us, Lord, for the days ahead.
May we be ever mindful that King Jesus is... Faithful and True.
He is our King now, and our soon-coming King!

*The wolf will live with the lamb, the leopard will lie down with
the goat, the calf and the lion and the yearling together;
and a little child will lead them.*
*In that day the Root of Jesse will stand as a banner for the
peoples; the nations will rally to him, and his place of rest
will be glorious.* (Isaiah 11:6, 10)

Enjoy His presence: still yourself, listen, write

September 7

Arrogance

Sovereign Lord, You are so Gracious to us.
All Authority and Power is Yours.
You are God, Most High.
Forgive us, Father, for our arrogant thinking…that our merits and strengths are
self-sufficient.
All our good works will not save us.
Your grace towards us is the Indescribable Gift of Your Son.
Jesus is the Way to righteousness before You, Holy God.
Help us to submit to Your Authority and Truth.
You alone can turn our filthy rags into robes of righteousness.
Forgive us for taking ourselves so seriously.
We praise You for Your Mercy.
Without You we are nothing.

The arrogant cannot stand in your presence. (Psalm 5:5)

Enjoy His presence: still yourself, listen, write

Hallelujah! Amen. It is Done.

September 8

Hold Our Hearts

Father, You are the Authority over all.
Even though we fight for control and think we have control, You are God Most High.
You are above all things.
Have mercy on us for bickering and fighting over political denominations.
Help us to resist the temptations in this world that comes with having power.
May we humbly submit to Your ways and to Your principles.
Open our hearts to the truth.
Create in us a desire to know Your Word.
Hold our hearts because our hearts can mislead us.
Help us not to forget You, or forsake You.
Hold our hearts, as we seek the Truth.

"Not by might nor by power, but by my Spirit," says the LORD Almighty. (Zec. 4:6)

Enjoy His presence: still yourself, listen, write

September 9

Faithful and True

Word of God, thank You for coming and dwelling among us.
Jesus is the Light of the world.
He is Faithful.
He is the Truth.
Holy Spirit of God, create in us a burning passion to know Your Word.
Help us respond to Your resurrection power that enables us to live out Your Word.
Help us not to keep the blessings and truth just to satisfy ourselves.
Instead, give us a willingness to sacrifice and be obedient.
May we respond to Your call to serve, and tell people the good news of the gospel.
Thank You, Father, for never giving up on us.
Your nature is to be... Faithful and True.
We praise You!

I saw heaven standing open and there before me was a white horse, whose rider is called Faithful and True. (Rev. 19:11)

Enjoy His presence: still yourself, listen, write

Hallelujah! Amen. It is Done.

Healing One

O God, You are the One that heals.
Thank You for sending us Jesus.
He is the Way to that good plan You have for us.
We need Him.
His presence is a Healing Balm.
No matter how deep the hurt, His Word can bring healing and peace.
Create in us a desire to know the truth written in the Bible.
Your Word gives us direction for healthy lifestyles.
Applying Your Word in our lives brings life to the fullest.
Help us to submit to Your Word.
Praise to Jesus...the Healing One.

He sent forth his word and healed them; he rescued them from the grave. Let them give thanks to the LORD for his unfailing love and his wonderful deeds for men. (Psalm 107:20-21)

Enjoy His presence: still yourself, listen, write

September 11

Firmly Attached

Father, You are the True Vine.
You give us life.
You provide us with everything we need to be fruitful and grow strong.
You are close.
You want more than anything else for us to be close to Your Son Jesus.
He is the Way to You...Holy God.
Help us to realize that we need Jesus.
Without Him we can do nothing.
Help us to surrender our lives to His ways and attach ourselves to Him.
Grant us the joy that comes from having a consistent close relationship with Jesus. Thank You, Father, for loving us so much. Thank You for the joy we can have when we are firmly attached to You.

"I am the vine; you are the branches. If a man remains in me and I in him, he will bear much fruit; apart from me you can do nothing." (John 15:5)

Enjoy His presence: still yourself, listen, write

Hallelujah! Amen. It is Done.

September 12

Ignorance

Father, You are Wise.
You give Wisdom.
You are Truthful.
Stop people from living a lie and doing the same thing over and over again.
Create in us a desire to start thinking and doing things differently.
Holy Spirit, give us the ability to recognize the difference between a lie and the truth.
We can find out and know what God says is true.
His Word is true.
Break through false thinking and bring us to the knowledge and truth about Jesus. He is...
the Way,
the Truth,
and the Life.

We demolish arguments and every pretension that sets itself up against the knowledge of God, and we take captive every thought to make it obedient to Christ. (2 Cor. 10:5)

Enjoy His presence: still yourself, listen, write

September 13

Bow

Father, Your Son Jesus is King.
He is a Wonderful Counselor and the Prince of Peace.
Every knee will bow someday at the sound of His Name.
Help us as we walk through our days, to bow to Him.
No matter what we face, may we walk in the awareness that we are walking with the King.
King Jesus wants to share His kingdom with us.
May we bow in humility, knowing that we can trust Him.
He is Merciful.
He is Sovereign.
He will lead us according to His great plan.
We bow down before our King.

But I, by your great mercy, will come into your house; in reverence will I bow down toward your holy temple. Lead me, O LORD, in your righteousness because of my enemies--make straight your way before me. (Psalm 5:7-8)

Enjoy His presence: still yourself, listen, write

Hallelujah! Amen. It is Done.

September 14

The Train

Come, Holy Spirit, revive us once again.
Create in us a desire to come honestly before You.
Help us to stop making excuses and agree with You about the areas of our lives that need to change.
Break through anything that gets in the way of us bowing to You.
Create in us a broken and contrite spirit.
Lord Jesus, come...
renew,
restore,
and revive Your Church.
Your kingdom come.
Your will be done.
Have mercy on us and release Your power!

And it will be said: "Build up, build up, prepare the road! Remove the obstacles out of the way of my people". For this is what the high and lofty One says---he who lives forever, whose name is holy: "I live in a high and holy place, but also with him who is contrite and lowly in spirit, to revive the spirit of the lowly and to revive the heart of the contrite." (Isaiah 57:14-15)

Enjoy His presence: still yourself, listen, write

September 15

Dancing Around the Ironing Board

You, Father, are the Joy-Giver.
You restore,
refresh,
and soothe.
You are Strength and Energy.
You are Fair and Trustworthy.
You know what's best for us.
You want the Light of Jesus in us to be more visible to those around us.
Becoming more like You and reflecting more and more of You is a lifetime process.
As You mold and shape us into Your image, there are times when we feel hard pressed.
You never said that being a Christian would be easy.
Remind us that Your love is Everlasting and You're right here with us.
Give us joy that only You can give.
Instill in us a sense of well-being.
Just like dancing, help us to joyfully follow Your lead, as You press out those areas of our lives that need to be more like You.
Thank You for the joy that You give, as we cling to You and look into Your eyes of grace.

"Do not grieve, for the joy of the LORD is your strength."
(Neh. 8:10)

Enjoy His presence: still yourself, listen, write

Hallelujah! Amen. It is Done.

September 16

Just in Time

Father, Your timing is perfect.
Thank You for protecting us in ways we're not even aware.
You are that Strong Tower we can run to for safety.
You protect us because You love us.
Help us to call on You in times of trouble.
Nothing is too big or too hopeless for You...Almighty God.
You gave us Jesus to save us, and we praise Him for His great Love and Obedience.
Open the eyes of Your people so they may see You protecting them in ways they can't explain.
May they know that You are Supernatural and working for them...just in time.

He will cover you with his feathers, and under his wings you will find refuge; his faithfulness will be your shield and rampart. (Psalm 91:4)

Enjoy His presence: still yourself, listen, write

Beauty

Lord Jesus, You are Beautiful.
Your Spirit is...
Loving,
Joyful,
Peaceful,
Patient,
Kind,
Good,
Faithful,
Gentle,
and Self-Controlled.
Your life taught us about true beauty.
You value beauty within, and not outward appearance.
Help us as we grow old to reflect Your unfading beauty of a gentle and quiet spirit.

Your beauty should not come from outward adornment, such as braided hair and the wearing of gold jewelry and fine clothes. Instead, it should be that of your inner self, the unfading beauty of a gentle and quiet spirit, which is of great worth in God's sight. (1 Peter 3:3-4)

Enjoy His presence: still yourself, listen, write

Hallelujah! Amen. It is Done.

September 18

Serving You

Father, You are worthy of all our praise.
You are Sympathetic.
You are Compassionate.
Give us teachable spirits so we may learn to serve Jesus to others.
Jesus taught us how to be humble servants.
Help us to be compassionate.
Give us a willingness to let go of our comfort, in order to bring comfort to others.
When we serve...
food for the hungry,
water for the thirsty,
hospitality for the stranger,
clothes for the needy,
care for the sick,
and visits to those in prison...we're really serving YOU!
Remind us that anything good in us comes from You.

"The King will reply, 'I tell you the truth, whatever you did for one of the least of these brothers of mine, you did for me.' " (Matt. 25:40)

Enjoy His presence: still yourself, listen, write

September 19

Stings Away!

Everlasting Father, Your Love is Relentless.
Your Love is wrapped around each one of our lives, guiding and guarding us.
You never turn Your head away from Your children.
You watch out for us all the time.
Your Love has no limit.
Thank You for taking the stings away caused by sin...
the sting of anger caused by hurt,
the sting of unforgiveness caused by abuse,
the sting of feeling worthless caused by neglect,
and the sting of anxiety caused by fear.
Loving Father, You have already provided victory over sin through our Savior, Jesus Christ.
Your children live in the hope found in Him.
With Jesus, the best is yet to come!

But thanks be to God! He gives us the victory through our Lord Jesus Christ. (1 Cor. 15:57)

Enjoy His presence: still yourself, listen, write

Hallelujah! Amen. It is Done.

September 20

Not Me First

Father, You are Creator.
You are the Master Potter, creating and shaping our lives.
It must sadden You when we resist Your Hands and turn our eyes from You.
Forgive us when we, or someone else, becomes more important than You.
Forgive us, Father, when we place...
our sexual desires,
our bodies,
and selfish pleasures before You.
Forgive us of our sin of idolatry.
Change our "me first" attitudes.
Change our hearts so we can say, "You first, Lord, not me first."
You are the Only One who can quench our thirsty and hungry souls.
Help us to use our bodies to honor You...our Creator.

But seek first his kingdom and his righteousness, and all these things will be given to you as well. (Matt. 6:33)

Enjoy His presence: still yourself, listen, write

September 21

I Will Acknowledge You

Father, You are the One True God.
Jesus is the One and Only.
He is Your Holy Spirit.
Your Word is true.
You cannot lie.
Lying is not in Your nature.
You said that Jesus is the Way, the Truth and the Life, and no one comes to You except through Him.
He is the Savior who You provided for us.
His Hand of grace is always extended.
Give Your people courage and boldness to tell people about Jesus.
Help them to be sensitive to Your leadings.
Hold back any form of discouragement in Your people when others say they don't want You.
We love You, Lord Jesus.
We acknowledge You as the One True God.

Whoever acknowledges me before men, I will also acknowledge him before my Father in heaven. (Matt. 10:32)

Enjoy His presence: still yourself, listen, write

Hallelujah! Amen. It is Done.

September 22

Shielded by God's Power

Jesus, our Lord and Savior, we praise You for constantly praying for us.

You are the Great Intercessor.

You are praying God's will for us.

Your will is the best, because You always have our best interests in mind.

Thank You for always thinking about us.

Thank You for always being available and ready to deliver and save.

Thank You that You hear us and know what we're going through.

Thank You for giving us Your Strength and Your Power, which enables us to walk through anything...because You're praying for us!

And he who searches our hearts knows the mind of the Spirit, because the Spirit intercedes for the saints in accordance with God's will. (Rom. 8:27)

Enjoy His presence: still yourself, listen, write

September 23

Wholeness of Children

Our Father, You are Trustworthy.
You are Faithful.
We praise You for...
Your completeness,
Your wholeness,
and for being everything we desperately need.
You used children as examples of how we are to trust in You.
In prayer we bring all people to You.
May people accept Jesus with a childlike faith and receive the spiritual wholeness of life forever with You.

Jesus said, "Let the little children come to me, and do not hinder them, for the kingdom of heaven belongs to such as these." (Matt. 19:14)

Enjoy His presence: still yourself, listen, write

Hallelujah! Amen. It is Done.

September 24

Try This

Lord Jesus, You are Kind.
You are Good.
You want all people to come to You and receive abundant life.
You're the Only One who won't let us down.
We can truly count on You.
Help Christians to keep going and never stop growing.
Push back discouragement and our desire to stay comfortable.
Help us to trust and obey You and daily get to know You more and more.
May we not be satisfied to just stay put and not grow with You.
Instead, may we daily try things Your way.
Open our eyes so we can see how Wonderful You are.

Taste and see that the LORD is good; blessed is the man who takes refuge in him. (Psalm 34:8)

Enjoy His presence: still yourself, listen, write

September 25

Holy Spirit, Come!

Father God, we praise Your Holy Spirit.
You are LORD God.
You are above all things, and You hold everything and everybody together.
Your Spirit cannot be contained or be controlled by mankind.
You are Sovereign.
You are King.
You are Most High.
Your Power is transforming.
Nothing is hopeless for You.
Come, Holy Spirit, and renew…
the lonely,
the desperate,
and the hard hearted.
You can change minds and hearts.
Praise to You for Your mercy and compassion.
Holy Spirit, come!
We need You.
We love You.

The Spirit and the bride say, "Come!" And let him who hears say, "Come!" Whoever is thirsty, let him come; and whoever wishes, let him take the free gift of the water of life. (Rev. 22:17)

Enjoy His presence: still yourself, listen, write

Hallelujah! Amen. It is Done.

September 26

Backseat Peacemakers

We praise You, Jesus, for being the Prince of Peace.
We want to be humble peacemakers.
In our marriages we want to give peace and be merciful.
Help us to speak positively about our spouses.
Enable us to see them through eyes of grace.
Teach husbands and wives about submitting to You, and to each other.
Give us humble hearts as we love one another.
We want our families to reflect Your Wisdom and Peace.
Strengthen our marriages.
Stretch out Your Hand and bless our marriages.
Help husbands and wives agree about raising their children.
May they also agree about the spending and saving of money.
But most of all, may they agree about You.

But the wisdom that comes from heaven is first of all pure; then peace-loving, considerate, submissive, full of mercy and good fruit, impartial and sincere. Peacemakers who sow in peace raise a harvest of righteousness. (James 3:17-18)

Enjoy His presence: still yourself, listen, write

Your Kingdom Come

We love You, Jesus.
You are the Best.
You are the Living Water.
You...
restore,
cleanse,
encourage,
and quench our thirsty souls.
Lord Jesus, strengthen Your people to be bright lights for You in
dark places.
Help them to feel Your presence.
Keep them healthy and guard them from anything that would
want to harm them as they participate in Your kingdom work.
Draw people to Yourself.
Have Your way.
Your kingdom come!

"Our Father in heaven, hallowed be your name, your
kingdom come, your will be done on earth as it is in
heaven." (Matt. 6:9-10)

Enjoy His presence: still yourself, listen, write

Hallelujah! Amen. It is Done.

September 28

No Rejection!

Father, praise to You for giving us Jesus.
He is our Atonement.
He is our Substitute for the punishment of sin.
He is the Only Way back to You.
May we never reject Him.
Forgive our arrogance when we think we don't need Him.
We do need Jesus.
Push back lies from the enemy and protect our minds.
Create in us a hunger for the truth of Your Word.
We appreciate You.
We are grateful for all You've done for us.
We love You, Lord Jesus.
You are so worthy of our praise.
Your Name is above all names...
High King,
Most High,
the Messiah...Jesus Christ.

"Whoever believes in the Son has eternal life, but whoever rejects the Son will not see life, for God's wrath remains on him." (John 3:36)

Enjoy His presence: still yourself, listen, write

September 29

I Believe

Father, You are Almighty.
You are the Creator of heaven and earth.
Jesus Christ is Your One and Only Son.
He is the Resurrection and the Life.
He is the Messiah,
the Lamb of God,
and the Truth.
Holy Spirit, draw all men, women and children to You.
Bring the truth about Jesus to all.
Holy Spirit, help people say..."Yes, Jesus, I believe You are Savior and Lord."

"Yes, Lord," she told him, "I believe that you are the Christ, the Son of God, who was to come into the world." (John 11:27)

Enjoy His presence: still yourself, listen, write

September 30

Open

Father, nothing is too hard for You.
No heart is too hard or mind too closed for You to change.
You can soften hearts and open minds to the truth about Jesus.
Melt away the lies, and bring a freedom found only in Jesus Christ.
Open our eyes so we can see the evidence of Jesus working in our lives.
Open our ears to hear the Truth.
Open our minds to Your transforming Word.
Open our hands to serve.
Melt away doubt and help us to respond to Jesus' invitation to come closer.
Mold and shape our lives with the truth.

What he opens no one can shut, and what he shuts no one can open. (Rev. 3:7)

Enjoy His presence: still yourself, listen, write

October

Photo by Cheryl Fairfield

Praise Him...*Hallelujah!*
Surrender to His will...*Amen.*
Live in faith as His plan unfolds...*It is done.*

October 1

Don't Go Back

Father, You are a Mighty Helper.
You are Powerful.
You are Most High.
Protect us from doubts that can weaken our trust in You.
Protect us from false teachers who distort Your Word.
Help us to respond to Your call to pray and study Your Word.
Holy Spirit of Truth, enable people to hold tight to the truth.
We need Your strength so we can move forward in Your truth.
By the power of Your Spirit help people to resist the temptation
to go back to old lies and old ways.

***It is the LORD your God you must follow, and him you must
revere. Keep his commands and obey him; serve him and
hold fast to him.*** (Deu. 13:4)

Enjoy His presence: still yourself, listen, write

Hallelujah! Amen. It is Done.

October 2

Healer for All Diseases

O God, praise Your Name forever.
Help us not to forget that no matter how we feel, You are still God.
You are the Great Physician.
Thank You for sending us Jesus, who ultimately heals all our diseases.
Thank You for Jesus' transforming power.
Help those that are sick...
physically,
emotionally,
or spiritually, to push forward to You.
Heal them Lord from...
lies,
fear,
bitterness,
and make them whole.
May they say..."Look what Jesus did. He really is the Son of God!"

For he had healed many, so that those with diseases were pushing forward to touch him. (Mark 3:10)

Enjoy His presence: still yourself, listen, write

October 3

Burning Hearts

Father God, You are like a Holy Fire.
You are All-Consuming.
You are Divine.
Holy Spirit of Truth, set a burning fire within each one of us to please You and obey You.
Create in us a divine passion to follow You.
Pour out Your Spirit, Your All-Consuming Fire on us.
Burn away lies and replace them with Your truth.
Give us burning hearts filled with a fresh desire to follow You.
Holy Spirit...relight the power of Your presence within us.

They asked each other, "Were not our hearts burning within us while he talked with us on the road and opened the Scriptures to us?" (Luke 24:32)

Enjoy His presence: still yourself, listen, write

Hallelujah! Amen. It is Done.

October 4

Upright

Father, You are the Upright One.
You are True,
Honest,
and Holy.
Thank You for holding on to us so we don't fall head long, or
too far.
You are the Shield.
You are God Most High, who provides the Way to save us.
Thank You for Jesus, who is...
the Way,
the Truth,
and the Life.
He keeps us upright when our walk is hard and each step is a
push.
He gives us joy even when life hurts and our circumstances are
not changing.
Help us as we walk in difficult times to keep going.
Enable us to rest along the way, in the joy of knowing that Jesus
is holding us upright.
He won't let go.

***The path of the righteous is level; O upright One, you make
the way of the righteous smooth.*** (Isaiah 26:7)

Enjoy His presence: still yourself, listen, write

October 5

Bend

Our Father, You are Lord God.
You know what is best for us.
Your plan for us is good and full of hope.
You want peace and order in our lives.
You want us to walk in truth and joy.
Help us, Holy Spirit, to respond to Your Strength, which is available to us because of our faith in Jesus.
Forgive us for trying to do things in our own strength.
Help us to bend to Your way, and humble ourselves.
You will lift us up.
Motivate us to change.
Open our minds so we can quickly see when we start to wander.
Thank You for always staying near us.
Help us to come near to You, and submit to Your ways.

Submit yourselves, then, to God. (James 4:7)

Enjoy His presence: still yourself, listen, write

Hallelujah! Amen. It is Done.

October 6

Merit

Father, how Great You are and worthy of our praise!
Thank You for giving us Jesus.
Father, You are Holy and cannot stand sin.
Jesus is the Perfect Way back to You.
Without Him we are lost.
Repenting and believing in Him brings eternal life.
Our accomplishments or achievements can never merit salvation.
It's by His grace we are saved.
Our merits here on earth fade, but the merit given to us through Jesus Christ lasts forever.

For it is by grace you have been saved, through faith---and this not from yourselves, it is the gift of God---not by works, so that no one can boast. (Eph. 2:8-9)

Enjoy His presence: still yourself, listen, write

October 7

Live Seed

Father, You are the Gardener.
You make everything grow.
You are the Power that takes the hard shell around a seed and softens it.
You are the Power that guides and lifts that seed through the hard ground.
You, Holy Spirit, can do the same thing in our lives.
You can soften hard and selfish hearts.
You can open stubborn and closed minds.
Your Power enables us to keep growing even when life seems hopeless and too hard.
Pour out Your Spirit upon us.
We want to live by the truth of Your Word.
Your Word endures forever.
The Power of Your Word brings life to dying souls.

For you have been born again, not of perishable seed, but of imperishable, through the living and enduring word of God. (1 Peter 1:23)

Enjoy His presence: still yourself, listen, write

Hallelujah! Amen. It is Done.

October 8

Atonement Cover

My God, we praise You for Your mercy.
Thank You that You don't keep score.
Each moment can be a new start with You.
All of us one day will have to choose where we will spend eternity.
Turn people around who are walking away from You.
Only Your Holy Spirit can bring the truth to their minds, the truth that Jesus paid the full price for our sins.
He took our place.
He gave His life for our lives.
His Blood covers our sins, so we can stand before You...Holy God.
Wash away arrogance and idolatry.
May we bow to Jesus, and get under His atonement covering.
Have mercy on us, Lord God.

If you, O LORD, kept a record of sins, O Lord, who could stand? But with you there is forgiveness; therefore you are feared. (Psalm 130:3-4)

Enjoy His presence: still yourself, listen, write

October 9

The Twist

Father, You are the Source of all Truth.
You are Truth itself.
You are the Upright One who is Faithful and True.
Your Holy Spirit never misleads us.
The truth is that You love us.
You sent Your One and Only Son Jesus, to save us.
Enable us to recognize any twist of the truth about Jesus.
Create in us a hunger to study Your Word.
For Your Word is flawless with no contradictions.
Jesus is the Living Word who is...
Pure,
Right,
Holy,
and True.

Sanctify them by the truth; your word is truth. (John 17:17)

Enjoy His presence: still yourself, listen, write

Hallelujah! Amen. It is Done.

October 10

Remember, God is God

Father God, You are Above All.
You alone are God Most High.
You are with us always, no matter how things look.
We are valuable to You.
You are...
before all things,
in the middle of all things,
and always there at the end of all things.
You are God, and there is no one like You.
Remembering who You are helps us not to worry or fret.
Your Word says You know what we need before we even ask.
You understand what we're going through and promise to never leave us.
Your Hand will pull us through.
Your Love is everlasting.
Help us, Jesus, to get our eyes off ourselves.
Help us to look at You and what You're doing.
We want to run to You first and then serve others.
You are God and we are not.

"Hallelujah! For the Lord God Almighty reigns." (Rev. 19:6)

Enjoy His presence: still yourself, listen, write

October 11

Wash Away

Father God, You provide everything we need to live in freedom.
You gave us Jesus.
His death unlocked the door of heaven for us.
Repenting of our sins and placing our faith in Jesus, sets us free from the grip of sin.
Jesus washes away the stain of our sins.
We need Jesus.
His Spirit enables us to overcome sin.
The more we get to know Jesus and His Power that lives within us, the more we are able to let go of anger and hurts.
In His time, He can change things.
He brings comfort, instead of anger.
He brings peace of mind, instead of guilt.
Jesus washes away our sins and sets us free.

So if the Son sets you free, you will be free indeed. (John 8:36)

Enjoy His presence: still yourself, listen, write

Hallelujah! Amen. It is Done.

October 12

Established

Holy God, You are Indescribable.

Words cannot adequately express or describe who You fully are.

One thing for sure...You do what You say You'll do.

Your Word is absolute truth.

You established Your Word to stand firm forever and to accomplish Your purpose and will.

You established the plan of salvation through Your Son, Jesus Christ.

You established Your Church and You're coming back for us soon.

You established prayer as a mighty weapon against the enemy.

You, O God are established as King forever.

Your reign is forevermore!

But the plans of the LORD stand firm forever, the purposes of his heart through all generations. (Psalm 33:11)

Enjoy His presence: still yourself, listen, write

October 13

His Love Is Ours

Father, Your Love is Extravagant.
You lavish Your Love upon us.
Your Love is beyond what our minds and hearts can take in.
You Love us so much that You gave us Your Only Son to die for our sins.
Agreeing with You about our sin,
placing our faith in Jesus,
and committing to follow Him secures our lives with You.
Your Love is willing to forgive.
You are interested in every detail of our lives.
You can bring joy in troubled times.
You can provide for our needs in ways we can't even explain.
You can take our empty lives and fill them with wonder and hope.
God is Love, and His Love is ours to have forever through Jesus Christ.

"For God so loved the world that He gave his one and only Son, that whoever believes in him shall not perish but have eternal life." (John 3:16)

Enjoy His presence: still yourself, listen, write

Hallelujah! Amen. It is Done.

October 14

Converted by God

O God, we praise You for Your transforming Power!
We see Your Power in...
the birth of a baby,
in lightning,
rain,
and wind.
We've seen Your Power change lives, for the alcoholic who no longer drinks,
and the drug addict who no longer desires to get high.
We've seen You bring peace to worried minds, and we've seen You restore broken marriages.
You can put our lives back together again.
You've given us our Only Hope...Jesus Christ.
His Spirit is the Power that enables people to change.
He is the Answer.
We can trust Him.
He wants to change things for us and bring us relief.
He makes things new.
Our prayer is for lives to be converted by God through Jesus Christ.

Therefore, if anyone is in Christ, he is a new creation; the old has gone, the new has come! (2 Cor. 5:17)

Enjoy His presence: still yourself, listen, write

October 15

Refresh Us

Praise You, Holy Spirit of God, for Your Mercy and Power.
You are able to make things different.
You can turn hopeless situations to hopeful days ahead.
You desire to cleanse us and restore us.
Your forgiveness and mercy brings freshness to our souls.
Open our minds and hearts so we will agree with You about the areas of our lives that need to be more like You.
Holy Spirit, breathe on us and create in us a passion to...
love You with all our...
hearts,
souls,
minds,
and strength.
We need You.
Refresh us, Lord.

Repent, then, and turn to God, so that your sins may be wiped out, that times of refreshing may come from the Lord. (Acts 3:19)

Enjoy His presence: still yourself, listen, write

Hallelujah! Amen. It is Done.

October 16

Keep Going

Blessed is Jesus, the King!
He is the Way and the Truth that brings life.
He is exactly who He said He is.
He is the One True God.
He alone brings peace.
We praise You!
Holy Spirit, empower Your precious servants who are in dark and desolate places to keep going.
May their...
smiles,
words,
families,
and lives be a bright reflection of You.
Protect them from anything or anybody that would want to harm them.
May they praise You and be filled with Your peace.
Father God, You alone are worthy of our praise!

"I tell you," he replied, "if they keep quiet, the stones will cry out." (Luke 19:40)

Enjoy His presence: still yourself, listen, write

October 17

Relational God

We praise You, Lord, for being our Intercessor.
Praying with You is an awesome blessing.
You are alive and Your Holy Spirit is living among us.
We praise You for being a Relational God.
It is amazing how You actually want to be with us, and share Your kingdom with us.
We are heirs of Yours.
Our inheritance is overflowing.
How Gracious and Generous You are.
You lavish Your Love upon us.
Thank You, Holy Spirit, for Your kindness and attention You give us.
Every breath we take we want to take in thanksgiving and praise to You...
our God,
our Father,
our Friend.

"Father, I want those you have given me to be with me where I am, and to see my glory, the glory you have given me because you loved me before the creation of the world." (John 17:24)

Enjoy His presence: still yourself, listen, write

Hallelujah! Amen. It is Done.

October 18

No Superficial Acclaims

Father, Your Word is...
True,
Trustworthy,
Alive,
and Flawless.
Jesus is the Word that came and dwelt among us.
He is the One who came to save us.
He is the Only One that grants peace with God.
He is the Messiah, the Christ.
Holy Spirit push back the lies that say Jesus was just a good teacher, or a good prophet.
Change minds and hearts to accept Jesus fully as Savior and Lord.
We can trust Him with our lives.
No superficial acclaims about Jesus...it's all of Him, not just what fits our standard of truth.
Jesus is the One True God.
Let us praise Him, because He is worthy of all praise!

Yet a time is coming and has now come when the true worshipers will worship the Father in spirit and truth, for they are the kind of worshipers the Father seeks. (John 4:23)

Enjoy His presence: still yourself, listen, write

October 19

Lift up Your Hands

Father God, thank You for Your Gracious Hands.
You are not afraid to get Your Hands dirty.
You will reach down and pull us up and out of some dirty messes.
The Hands of Jesus are extended to all sinners.
No one is good enough to stand before a Holy God.
Help us to lift up our hands in surrender, agreeing that we have sinned and done You wrong.
Only the Blood of Jesus can wash away the sins on our dirty hands.
He makes us clean and doesn't keep score of our sins.
Thank You for Your Hands of forgiveness and grace.
Let us lift up our hands in praise and thanksgiving.

I will praise you as long as I live, and in your name I will lift up my hands. (Psalm 63:4)

Enjoy His presence: still yourself, listen, write

Hallelujah! Amen. It is Done.

October 20

Jaded, Yet Never Too Tough

Father, we praise You for being a Zealous God.
You are passionate about changing our lives so we may experience Your peace in tough circumstances.
You know all about feeling...
rejected,
alone,
angry,
and hurt.
Help us to allow You to melt our icy emotions and soften our slowly hardened heart.
Turn us from memories that make us bitter and angry.
May we allow You to enlighten our minds with Your wisdom and peace.
Help us to have hearts that are tender toward You.
Thank You, Father, that Your Power is able to change minds and hearts.
No one is too tough for You.

The zeal of the LORD Almighty will accomplish this. (Isaiah 9:7)

Enjoy His presence: still yourself, listen, write

October 21

Now, Before It's Too Late

Father, You created us and purposely placed us in life at this specific time.
May our lives on earth really count.
Help us to come to the truth as to why we were created in the first place.
Because of Your great Love You created us.
You want us to be with You forever.
But sin separates us from You, because You are Holy.
The Only Way we can be with You forever is by turning from our sins and placing our faith in Jesus.
His Blood paid the price for our sins.
He is the Way to the Father.
He is the Truth.
He gives us Life.
Holy Spirit, stop people from continuing to put off Jesus.
Help them to quit resisting who He really is.
May they choose Jesus, now, before it's too late.
Take away the lies and clearly bring the truth into their thinking.
Help people to clearly understand and accept by faith that the Only Way we will live forever is through Jesus Christ.

I tell you, now is the time of God's favor, now is the day of salvation. (2 Cor. 6:2)

Enjoy His presence: still yourself, listen write

Hallelujah! Amen. It is Done.

October 22

Crossroad

Father, Your Way is Good.
In this world we are exposed to so many fakes and lies.
Help people to see and recognize the Only True Way back to You.
Stir in them a curiosity to know the truth about Jesus.
Bring people to that crossroad in their lives where a decision has to be made about Jesus.
We will spend eternity in one of two places…heaven or hell.
Clear the minds of people from all the clutter that pulls them away from the Truth.
Cut through confusion and deceit.
Help them respond to Your call to accept the Only Way that gives true rest for their weary souls.
Your Way gives life forever.

This is what the LORD says: "Stand at the crossroads and look; ask for the ancient paths, ask where the good way is, and walk in it, and you will find rest for your souls." (Jer. 6:16)

Enjoy His presence: still yourself, listen, write

October 23

Light and Dark

Father, darkness isn't even dark to You.
You can take what seemingly looks like a horrible situation and bring relief.
Jesus is the Light in a dark world.
He is Real,
Right
and True.
Darkness doesn't like to be around the Light.
Jesus overcame darkness so we could live in the Light.
As children of God, we can live in victory.
We can have joy and peace in the middle of any affliction.
Shine Your Light on all who are afflicted and oppressed.
May they feel Your Hand as they walk in Your comforting Light.
Thank You, Jesus, for Your Light in this world.

When Jesus spoke again to the people, he said, "I am the light of the world. Whoever follows me will never walk in darkness, but will have the light of life." (John 8:12)

Enjoy His presence: still yourself, listen, write

Hallelujah! Amen. It is Done.

October 24

Divided by Lies

Father, You are LORD God.
There is nothing, or no one, greater than You.
You are the True God.
You do not and cannot lie.
You are Relational too.
More than anything else, You want us to be with You.
Your Gift of Grace comes with the invitation to...
repent,
believe,
and live forever!
You love us so much that You provided for us the Only Way
back to You, and that's through Your Son, Jesus.
Good deeds, going to church, or trying to live right won't give
us a saving relationship with You.
We cannot save ourselves.
Free people from the lies that say, if they...
treat people right,
follow set rules,
or abide by traditions they will earn salvation.
Unite us in truth and protect us from being divided by lies.

**But the LORD is the true God; he is the living God, the
eternal King.** (Jer. 10:10)

Enjoy His presence: still yourself, listen, write

October 25

Preserve

Thank You, Father, that You preserve our lives through Jesus.
You have graciously given Him to us.
The power of His Blood...
forgives us,
helps us to forget past hurts,
doesn't keep score,
and doesn't accuse us.
Make us more like You.
We want our lives to reflect Your presence within us.
Help us to be a preservative that brings out the best in others.
Give us kind words to say.
Make us patient listeners.
Give us the desire to encourage others, and the discipline to pray for others.
Thanks again for preserving our lives through Jesus Christ.

"For God so loved the world that he gave his one and only Son, that whoever believes in him shall not perish but have eternal life." (John 3:16)

Enjoy His presence: still yourself, listen, write

Hallelujah! Amen. It is Done.

October 26

His Time

Lord, Your ways and Your timing are not like ours.
You have the plan, the best plan for our lives.
Lord Jesus, free us from the mind-set of time.
Free us from anything that creates anxiety in us or causes us to hurry.
Remove the feeling of not having enough time.
Take away the sadness of time lost in the past.
Remind us that You can make up for lost time.
Once again, bring to our minds that You are in control.
You are the Time Keeper.
You don't need a watch or a calendar.
Help us not to get in Your way.
Help us to wait on You and not press things too fast or move too slow.
We want Your pace.
Help us to trust Your timing.
You are the Prince of Peace and Your timing is perfect.

He has made everything beautiful in its time. (Ecc. 3:11)

Enjoy His presence: still yourself, listen, write

October 27

In Him

Jesus, You are Savior and Lord.
You are the One True God.
You know how difficult life can be.
You know what it's like to be...
alone, rejected, stressed, and afraid.
You truly understand what we're going through.
Your Love for us is unfailing.
There is nothing like having the Gift of a personal relationship
with Jesus, and growing to know Him more and more.
Near His heart is a place of quiet comfort and joy.
In Jesus, we can...
rest in Him,
grow in Him,
trust in Him,
and overcome in Him.

*"I am the vine; you are the branches. If a man remains in
me and I in him, he will bear much fruit; apart from me you
can do nothing."* (John 15:5)

Enjoy His presence: still yourself, listen, write

Hallelujah! Amen. It is Done.

October 28

Manna

Great God, You are the Faithful Provider.
You give us each day exactly what we need.
You strengthen us with joy.
Your grace is sufficient.
Your timing is perfect.
We can completely trust You.
You are…
Faithful,
Reliable,
and Truthful.
Each day help us to trust You more and more.
Bring scriptures to our minds that encourage our souls.
Help us to rest in Your strength.
Give us Your joy that never runs out.
Thank You for giving us everything we need through Jesus Christ.

And my God will meet all your needs according to his glorious riches in Christ Jesus. (Phil. 4:19)

Enjoy His presence: still yourself, listen, write

October 29

Sweet Fire

Holy Spirit, fall upon us each day.
Each step we take, give us a fresh anointing of Your Power.
Holy Spirit, we thank You for Your Power within us, the power to overcome darkness of any kind.
Your Power enables us to face challenges that are way too big for us.
The sweet fire of Your presence enables us to...
forgive the deepest hurt,
give up our right to be understood,
manage the pain,
face the truth,
and say good-bye to a loved one.
You are the Strength within us.
Remind us that we are more than conquerors.
We are dressed in Your garment of righteousness.
We are set apart and marked by Jesus.
The sweet fire of Your presence strengthens us, and keeps us steady, as we walk in joyful obedience.

Who is it that overcomes the world? Only he who believes that Jesus is the Son of God. (1 John 5:5)

Enjoy His presence: still yourself, listen write

Hallelujah! Amen. It is Done.

October 30

Your Bride

Father, You are coming back for Your Bride.
What a great day that will be!
We are Your Bride and Jesus is the Bridegroom.
You want us to be with You.
Thank You, Jesus, for teaching us about the Love of our Father.
Thank You for loving us before we even knew You.
Your Love…
never changes,
keeps promises,
saves,
encourages,
protects,
strengthens,
and is forevermore!
Holy Spirit, continue to shape and mold us into Your Bride.
We want to be prepared and ready when You come for us.
We're waiting with joyful anticipation!
You love us.
We…Your Bride…love You!

Let us rejoice and be glad and give him glory! For the wedding of the Lamb has come, and his bride has made herself ready. (Rev. 19:7)

Enjoy His presence: still yourself, listen, write

October 31

Our Nutrient

Father, You are everything we need.
You are Good.
You are Gracious.
You are Strong.
You strengthen us with Your Word.
Your Word is sweet.
Your Word is powerful.
Your Word is everlasting.
Help us to spiritually grow strong and healthy.
You are the nourishment that sustains us forever.
Open hearts and minds to willingly receive Your Son, Jesus.
He is the Nutrient, which our hungry souls need.

Taste and see that the LORD is good; blessed is the man who takes refuge in Him. (Psalm 34:8)

Enjoy His presence: still yourself, listen, write

Hallelujah! Amen. It is Done.

November

Photo by Judy Elmer

Praise Him...*Hallelujah!*
Surrender to His will...*Amen.*
Live in faith as His plan unfolds...*It is done.*

November 1

I Am Not Leaving

Father, thank You for Your Word.
You keep Your Word.
You said You'll never leave us.
You're with us every moment of our days, and every step that we take.
No matter what we're going through, or where we are, You're not leaving.
You said so.
You're not leaving us in the bad times, like...
losing a loved one,
chemotherapy treatment,
or a spouse who doesn't love us anymore.
And You're not leaving us in the good times, like...
our wedding day,
the birth of a baby,
or when the doctor's report comes back benign.
Help us to reach out to Jesus.
He's the Light that shows us the Way.
Thank You for Your Love and Faithfulness.
Remind us each day... You're not leaving us.

"And surely I am with you always, to the very end of the age." (Matt. 28:20)

Enjoy His presence: still yourself, listen, write

Hallelujah! Amen. It is Done.

November 2

Again, Less

Our Father, we praise You for Your Patience and Love.
You are a Gracious God, and we're thankful.
Help us not to take advantage of Your Goodness towards us.
May we boldly respond to Your enabling Power.
We are called to be holy and set apart.
The Holy Spirit gives us...
the power to change,
the power to overcome temptation,
and the power to stop doing things over and over again that displeases You.
Help us to respond to Your transforming power.
Help us to be willing to go through the pressure and pain that sometime comes with change.
Pour out Your Spirit, which enables us to boldly say "No" to sin.
We want more of You and less of us.
We praise You for Your sanctifying grace.

But where sin increased, grace increased all the more. (Rom. 5:20)

Enjoy His presence: still yourself, listen, write

November 3

His Sheep

Lord, You are the Good Shepherd.
You watch out for us and take care of us.
Your presence within us is more powerful than any power in this world.
We are connected to You.
When troubles want to scatter us, help us to run to Your Word.
Your Word is Your voice.
Your sheep can recognize and hear Your voice.
There is great joy when we sense You speaking to our hearts.
Help us to stay close.
We can easily wander.
Help us to follow Your lead.
Your will for us is good.
Your way is the best!

When he has brought out all his own, he goes on ahead of them, and his sheep follow him because they know his voice. (John 10:4)

Enjoy His presence: still yourself, listen, write

Hallelujah! Amen. It is Done.

November 4

Send Forth Your Spirit

Father, words cannot adequately express how grateful we are that You sent Jesus to save us, and Your Holy Spirit to guide us.
We praise You for Your Love and Faithfulness.
Send forth Your Spirit.
Fill us up with Your wisdom,
Guide us in the truth.
Empower us to be obedient.
Humble us to accept Your corrections.
Open us to Your comfort and peace.
May we never forget that Your Powerful Spirit lives within believers today.
In the power of Your Spirit send us!

Send forth your light and your truth, let them guide me.
(Psalm 43:3)

Enjoy His presence: still yourself, listen, write

November 5

Bloodthirsty

Father, You see everything.
You know what Your children are going through.
Your eyes see their hurts and persecution.
You hear the lies said against them.
You will take action against those who hurt Your children.
You are a Just God and the Judge.
Reassure Your children living in these horrible situations that You have not forgotten them.
You are a Zealous God.
You are the Deliverer.
Give them the strength that only You can give.
Remind them, Lord, that You are near.
Your Blood covers them and saves them.
Encourage them that their Deliverer is coming.
The best is yet to come!

Deliver me from my enemies, O God; protect me from those who rise up against me. Deliver me from evildoers and save me from bloodthirsty men. (Psalm 59:1-2)

Enjoy His presence: still yourself, listen, write

Hallelujah! Amen. It is Done.

November 6

Sexual Impurity

Father, You have called us to be different from the world.
We live in this world, but we don't have to be a part of those
things that are displeasing to You.
You have created our bodies to be honorable and holy.
Help us to control our selfish desires.
Help us to realize that this life is not all about what makes us feel
good.
Protect the young people from the world's immoral lies found in
the lyrics of some music.
Create in us the desire to know You.
You are the Only One that can bring lasting...
contentment,
satisfaction,
and joy.

**It is God's will that you should be sanctified: that you should
avoid sexual immorality; that each of you should learn to
control his own body in a way that is holy and honorable,
not in passionate lust like the heathen, who do not know
God.** (1 Thess. 4:3-5)

Enjoy His presence: still yourself, listen, write

November 7

Full of Grace and Truth

Father, You are God.
There is no one, or anything, above You.
Your thoughts and ways are higher than ours.
You are the Highest.
You are the Truth.
Forgive us for thinking that we, who were made from dust, can somehow be equal to You.
Forgive us for placing our abilities and strength above Yours.
Forgive us for thinking that the knowledge we've gained is by our power.
Forgive us for developing our own way.
Jesus is the Way.
His nail-scarred Hands are extended to all people.
His Hands are full of Grace and Truth.

The Word became flesh and made his dwelling among us. We have seen his glory, the glory of the One and Only, who came from the Father, full of grace and truth. (John 1:14)

Enjoy His presence: still yourself, listen, write

Hallelujah! Amen. It is Done.

November 8

Heat Produces Change

Father, You want the very best for us.
You want us to become stronger and stronger and grow to trust You more and more.
Help us to remember that You are with us all the time.
Bring to our minds that You are near, especially during the hard times.
Strengthen us when we feel like You've turned the "heat" up on high in our lives.
We pray against discouragement as we wait on You to make things better.
Help us during these times of suffering and struggles to hear You whisper...
"I am here."
Remind us that You will not take Your eyes off us.
Change our minds and hearts.
Create in us a new attitude.
Help us to cling to You.
Create in us the strength to keep going.
Our hope is in You.

Not only so, but we also rejoice in our sufferings, because we know that suffering produces perseverance; perseverance, character; and character, hope. (Rom. 5:3-4)

Enjoy His presence: still yourself, listen, write

November 9

I Understand

Jesus, You are Compassionate.
You feel and know our pain.
You hold us with kind and patient Hands.
You listen and understand everything we're going through.
You care.
You were rejected.
You experienced the loss of loved ones.
And You experienced being alone, as You died on that cross for us.
Help us to remember that because of our faith in You that same power that raised You from the dead is the power within us.
You are able to change our lives.
You restore, and bring peace and joy, in horrible circumstances.
You are our Hope, no matter how hopeless things feel.
Help us not to run away from You.
But instead, run to You, because…You understand.

Jesus wept. (John 11:35)

Enjoy His presence: still yourself, listen, write

Hallelujah! Amen. It is Done.

November 10

Your Fingerprint

Loving Father, Your plan for us involves a great inheritance with rewards.

Because of our repentance of sin and faith in Jesus, we are Your children and belong to Your family.

We are blood relatives because of Your Precious Blood.

Thank You that we are identified with Jesus.

Father, help us each day to look more like Jesus and less like us.

Create in us a desire to be obedient.

Knock away any form of fear or doubt.

Take our hands and place them in Your Hands.

We choose to go in the direction You want us to go.

Thank You for Your Mighty hold on us.

Father, we want Your Fingerprint on everything we do.

May the favor of the Lord our God rest upon us; establish the work of our hands for us--- yes, establish the work of our hands. (Psalm 90:17)

Enjoy His presence: still yourself, listen, write

November 11

Waiting With You

Our Father, thank You for never leaving us, no matter how bad things get.
Thank You for never getting in a hurry with us.
You're always willing to listen.
Holy Spirit, strengthen the men and women who are serving in the armed forces.
Bless them as they sacrifice their time.
It's hard to give the time up from family and friends.
Use this time in their lives as an opportunity to come to Jesus and serve others.
You showed us how to be humble servants when You walked this earth.
Help us to patiently serve others.
Make us willing to wait on others.
Increase in us an awareness of Your presence, as we wait with You.

Wait for the LORD; be strong and take heart and wait for the LORD. (Psalm 27:14)

Enjoy His presence: still yourself, listen, write

Hallelujah! Amen. It is Done.

November 12

Laughter

Father, thank You for laughter that...
makes us feel better,
relieves tension,
and helps us put things in the proper perspective.
Thank You, Father, that You laugh.
You created laughter because it's good for us.
Instill in us laughter that is uplifting to our souls, even when our hearts ache.
Help us not to take our circumstances and ourselves so seriously.
Give us the blessing of laughter when husbands and wives get upset with each other.
Fill relationships with Your peace and joy.

Our mouths were filled with laughter, our tongues with songs of joy. (Psalm 126:2)

Enjoy His presence: still yourself, listen, write

November 13

Enduring the Heat

Father, You are God Almighty.
Nothing is impossible, or too far gone for You.
When we find ourselves in deep trouble or anxiety running high,
help us to turn to You.
Break in us any stubbornness to keep doing things in our own
strength.
Help us during times of testing and pain, to invite You to come
help.
May we never push You away.
You are the Strength needed to endure and keep going.
Your Comfort sustains us.
May we respond to Your soothing presence that protects and
saves.

*"When you pass through the waters, I will be with you;
and when you pass through the rivers, they will not sweep
over you. When you walk through the fire, you will not
be burned; the flames will not set you ablaze. For I am
the LORD, your God, the Holy One of Israel, your Savior."*
(Isaiah 43:2-3)

Enjoy His presence: still yourself, listen, write

Hallelujah! Amen. It is Done.

November 14

Peacefully Together

Father, true peace comes from knowing that You are in control.
We try so hard to be self-reliant, yet Christ-reliant is the answer.
We try to do so much in our own strength.
Apart from You we can do nothing.
Forgive us, Father, of our self-centeredness.
Help us to always place You in the center of our lives.
Help us to give You first place in our minds and hearts.
Create in us a hunger for Your Word.
Stir in us a desire to come to You in prayer.
Give us a keen sense of discernment so we choose our friends
wisely.
Guard us from temptations of the world.
For You, Lord Jesus, can bring a peace to us that no one can
really understand.
May the Prince of Peace hold us peacefully together with Him.

***And the peace of God, which transcends all understanding,
will guard your hearts and your minds in Christ Jesus.*** (Phil. 4:7)

Enjoy His presence: still yourself, listen, write

My Umpire

Lord, You are God.
You know everything about our situation.
You know us better than we know ourselves.
You always have our best interests in mind.
You're always watching and listening to us.
Not for one second do You stop loving us.
Help us to submit to Your plan and Your call in our lives.
Increase our trust in You, so we will let You call the shots in our lives.
Create in us a passion to know You more.
Give us the desire to live our lives by what You say.
Enable us to stop living our lives in our own strength.
May we place You first.
May we live our lives respecting Your Word as the final word.

Nothing in all creation is hidden from God's sight. (Heb. 4:13)

Enjoy His presence: still yourself, listen, write

Hallelujah! Amen. It is Done.

November 16

God Knows

Thank You, Father, for fighting for us.
Your Word says that You are a Warrior and the battle is Yours.
Give us peace, Lord, when we've been…
falsely accused,
criticized,
or mocked.
Remind us that You are God and You know what's going on.
Give us Your Power that enables us to control our tongue and actions when the battle continues on.
Help us to stand firm and rest in the Power of Christ.
You know the truth about what we're going through.
Bring us peace in knowing that…God knows.

"This is what the LORD says to you: 'Do not be afraid or discouraged because of this vast army. For the battle is not yours, but God's.'" (1 Chr. 20:15)

Enjoy His presence: still yourself, listen, write

First Place

Jesus is Lord over all.
He is before all things.
Lord God, thank You for creating us in Your universe.
We praise You for the blessing of life.
You, O Lord, are the Authority.
Help us to put You in first place in our lives.
Forgive us when we place ourselves ahead of You.
Help us to submit to Your Supremacy.
For our lives are blessings from Your Creating Hands.
You are Most High…and we are not.

He is before all things, and in him all things hold together.
(Col. 1:17)

Enjoy His presence: still yourself, listen, write

Hallelujah! Amen. It is Done.

November 18

God Smiles

Father, You created each one of us according to Your image.
Thank You for creating in us an ability to smile.
If we can smile, You must smile, too.
Smiles can make such a difference in our attitudes.
Thank You for...
a baby's first smile,
an elderly person's smile through a wrinkled face,
and the innocent smile of a special-needs adult.
Help us, Lord, to give our smiles away.
With Your help we can smile, even when we don't understand
why things happen the way they do.
Father, remind people of Your Great Love for them.
Bring back smiles in the faces of those who feel they've lost
their ability to smile.

*The LORD make his face shine upon you and be gracious
to you; the LORD turn his face toward you and give you
peace.* (Num. 6:25-26)

Enjoy His presence: still yourself, listen, write

Spring of Water

Father, without You we are dead...living, yet dead.
Without You, our lives are spiraling downward.
But You, Father, have provided the Way for us to be with You and live a life of blessings, a life lived with a personal relationship with Jesus.
His Holy Spirit enables us to live life to the fullest.
We can have His power and peace in times of great pain and intense struggles.
Jesus is that Spring of Water that can...
free us,
save us,
and cleanse us.
His Spirit empowers us to change, even when we feel change could never happen. Restore and refresh us, Lord Jesus.
You give abundant life.

"Indeed, the water I give him will become in him a spring of water welling up to eternal life." (John 4:14)

Enjoy His presence: still yourself, listen, write

Hallelujah! Amen. It is Done.

November 20

Bottom Line

Gracious Father, You are Number One.
You are Most High.
You are Above All.
You are God and we are not.
Father, forgive us for our pride and arrogance.
Forgive us for thinking that we are doing things in our own strength.
The truth is Jesus Christ is our Strength.
Bottom line, He is the Way, and there is no other person or way to the Father except through Him.
You said so.
Jesus is Your Gracious plan of salvation for us.
Help us not to exchange the truth for a lie.
Bottom line...someday every knee will bow and every tongue will confess that Jesus Christ is Lord.

Therefore God exalted him to the highest place and gave him the name that is above every name, that at the name of Jesus every knee should bow, in heaven and on earth and under the earth, and every tongue confess that Jesus Christ is Lord, to the glory of God the Father. (Phil. 2:9-11)

Enjoy His presence: still yourself, listen, write

November 21

My Redeemer

We love You, Lord God.
You are Holy.
You are Powerful.
You care.
You want us with You, to the extent that You gave Your life for us.
You are everywhere at all times.
No place is too hard for You to get to.
Your presence is Powerful, so powerful that hearts and minds can change.
By the Power of Your Spirit, make Your presence real and alive for those that are dying alone in horrible conditions.
You are the Pain-Reliever.
You are the Prince of Peace.
You are the Redeemer.
Bring people to the point where they agree about their sins, and say in faith...
"Yes, my Redeemer lives!"

I know my Redeemer lives, and that in the end he will stand upon the earth. (Job 19:25)

Enjoy His presence: still yourself, listen, write

Hallelujah! Amen. It is Done.

November 22

For the Weak and Lonely

Loving Father, You are near.
You never step away from our side.
You stand beside us.
We are never alone.
Remove the lie that says we are too weak and lonely to count.
You think differently.
You look for the weak, so Your Power will be evident.
Help us to simply trust Your Word.
You are Faithful and Strong.
You say You will never leave us.
That's a promise.
Help us, Father, to feel Your presence and live in Your Power.
Thank You for hearing our prayers.

The prayer of a righteous man is powerful and effective.
(James 5:16)

Enjoy His presence: still yourself, listen, write

Your Temple

Father, You are so Good to us.
You created us in so many wonderful ways.
Our bodies are a miracle made by You.
When we repent and believe in Jesus, Your Spirit lives within our bodies.
We are humbled.
Our bodies become temples of Your Holy Spirit.
Forgive us when we use our bodies for selfish reasons.
Forgive us for dishonoring You.
Help us not to do anything sexually immoral that would dishonor Your presence within us.
As believers we have Your Power that enables us to say "no" to sexual immorality.
Help us not to get caught up in the lie that a little bit won't hurt.
Free us from the attraction to satisfy our selfish desires.
Help us to honor You with our bodies.

Do you not know that your body is a temple of the Holy Spirit, who is in you, whom you have received from God? You are not your own; you were bought at a price. Therefore honor God with your body. (1 Cor. 6:19-20)

Enjoy His presence: still yourself, listen, write

Hallelujah! Amen. It is Done.

November 24

Yielding to the Potter's Hands

Father, You are the Master Potter.
Your Loving Hands can change things.
Help us daily to yield to Your Spirit.
Your plan for us is better than anything we could ever plan.
Help us to trust You as our lives change.
Take away any fear that sometimes come with change.
Free our minds to allow You to mold and shape our lives, so we
may experience You more abundantly.
Nothing is too out of shape or too far gone for You to restore.
Help us to grow, instead of being contained in one spot.
Instill in us a willingness to yield to Your Hands.
Move us closer and closer to You.
We choose to be like clay in Your Loving Hands.

"O house of Israel, can I not do with you as this potter
does?" declares the LORD. "Like clay in the hand of
the potter, so are you in my hand, O house of Israel."
(Jer. 18:6-7)

Enjoy His presence: still yourself, listen, write

November 25

He Will Come

Jesus is coming…He promised!
He will be back.
May people open up the Bible and read Your words of hope.
Push back anything that keeps people from reading Your Word.
Awake in us a hunger and deep desire to know Jesus.
Open our minds and hearts to the Truth.
Father, prepare us for Your coming.
Make us ready for Jesus.
He will come.
He said He would.
He keeps His promises!

"Behold, I am coming soon! Blessed is he who keeps the words of the prophecy in this book." (Rev. 22:7)

Enjoy His presence: still yourself, listen, write

Hallelujah! Amen. It is Done.

Shut In

Our Father, thank You for loving Your children with a Protective Hand.
Your Hand cannot be turned back.
Nothing can separate Your children from Your love that is in Jesus Christ.
Your love is...Ever Present, and Never Ending.
Your children run to You for safety.
You are...
our Deliverer,
our Provider,
and our Encourager.
What comfort it is to know that we are surrounded by Your presence and shut in.

The animals going in were male and female of every living thing, as God had commanded Noah. Then the LORD shut him in. (Gen. 7:16)

Enjoy His presence: still yourself, listen, write

November 27

Heavy Steps

Dearest Jesus, You are the Strength we need.
You uphold us when the pressures of this world make us feel like we're going under.
Help us, Lord, not to get stuck in our troubles.
Give us the strength to run the course You've laid out for us.
As the days and years pass and our steps become labored and heavy, help us to turn to You.
Your Power restores us and enables us to keep going.
Refresh us, O Lord, as we follow You.
Help us to always walk closely with You.
Thank You, Jesus, for being with us every step of the way.
We can rest in You.

"Come to me, all you who are weary and burdened, and I will give you rest. Take my yoke upon you and learn from me, for I am gentle and humble in heart, and you will find rest for your souls." (Matt. 11:28-29)

Enjoy His presence: still yourself, listen, write

Hallelujah! Amen. It is Done.

November 28

Clay in Your Hands

Our God, we praise You for Your transforming power.
You are the Divine Potter.
You give Grace
You bring Hope.
You don't get in a hurry with us.
Just like the clay on the potter's wheel, You patiently...
prepare us,
center us,
open us,
and pull us up.
Help us to submit each day to Your will.
May we be like clay in Your Hands.
Help us to rest in Your Hands as our lives change.
Make us more like You.
Thank You for Your Loving Hands that holds us tight.

"Like clay in the hand of the potter, so are you in my hand, O house of Israel." (Jer. 18:6)

Enjoy His presence: still yourself, listen, write

November 29

Look Where You've Come From

Holy Spirit, thank You for Your peace.
Thank You for guidance and forgiveness.
Help us to stay centered and focused on the Prize.
Make us aware of how You give us what we need.
Thank You for bringing us this far.
Help us not to go back, or slip back to an old way that's displeasing to You.
We ask for Your continued...
protection,
guidance,
and strength to keep looking ahead, to You, Our Jesus.
We also ask for wisdom and discernment.
We want to be able to quickly recognize any distraction, or any form of deceit from the enemy.
Thank You, Father, for everything...
You've done,
are doing,
and are about to do in our lives.

Brothers, I do not consider myself yet to have taken hold of it. But one thing I do: Forgetting what is behind and straining toward what is ahead, I press on toward the goal to win the prize for which God has called me heavenward in Christ Jesus. (Phil. 3:13-14)

Enjoy His presence: still yourself, listen, write

Hallelujah! Amen. It is Done.

November 30

Taking Us Through

Father, You can make things so much better for us.
Your Love is greater than anything this world could ever offer.
Because of Your Great Love, You gave us Jesus.
He is the Door to saving grace.
A personal relationship with Jesus is the Way to walk through life.
His Spirit enables us to take one step at a time, even when we can't see where we're going.
Help us, Father, to fully rely on Him.
Help us to remember that...
in good times and bad times,
in highs and lows,
with blessings and sufferings,
and when life opens and closes, You are always with us...taking us through.

"And surely I am with you always, to the very end of the age." (Matt. 28:20)

Enjoy His presence: still yourself, listen, write

December

Photo by Cheryl Fairfield

Praise Him...*Hallelujah!*
Surrender to His will...*Amen.*
Live in faith as His plan unfolds...*It is done.*

December 1

You Are Divine

Holy God, You are Perfect.
In all Your ways You are LORD God.
Perfection is Your standard.
We praise You for sending Jesus, the Perfect Way.
Jesus, who was both human and divine, gave up His life for us.
He experienced death by crucifixion.
He rose from the dead.
He is alive.
He is Grace.
He is the Only One who provides the Way home to You.
Lord God...You are Divine.
We are not.

God said to Moses, "I AM WHO I AM." "This is my name forever, the name by which I am to be remembered from generation to generation." (Ex. 3:14,15)

Enjoy His presence: still yourself, listen, write

Hallelujah! Amen. It is Done.

December 2

The Builder

Father, we praise You that You're not afraid to get Your Hands dirty.

You shape and mold us like the potter does the clay.

We are formed into Your likeness and for Your purpose.

You see us as finished vessels.

Nothing in our lives is too heavy, or too dirty for You to push back or move aside. You don't tear us down.

You are the Builder.

You are the Greatest Encourager.

Help us not to get discouraged or downhearted as we see our shortcomings.

Give us patience as we realize that change takes time.

You never get in a hurry with us.

You are Patient.

You are Compassionate.

Remind us that Your Holy Spirit builds us up!

For every house is built by someone, but God is the builder of everything. (Heb. 3:4)

Enjoy His presence: still yourself, listen, write

December 3

All the Pieces

Father, You are God Almighty.
Your Power never weakens.
You are Secure and Stable.
Nothing changes You.
We can trust You completely.
Your Love for us is everlasting.
You care deeply for us.
You stand with us.
You are interested in all the pieces of our lives.
Nothing is insignificant in Your eyes.
You can take what looks impossible and overwhelming, and bring order and peace.
You are able to bring wisdom and understanding to situations where we struggle for answers.
You help us to know where to take the next step.
Help us to bring all the broken pieces of our lives to Jesus.
He will guide us and hold us, as He puts us back together again.

He is before all things, and in him all things hold together.
(Col. 1:17)

Enjoy His presence: still yourself, listen, write

Hallelujah! Amen. It is Done.

December 4

Dead to Alive

Thank You, Father, for providing a means of escape.
Without Jesus we are like dead people walking.
But with Him we can have life forever.
Salvation is through no one else but Jesus Christ.
He is the Gift of Grace given to us by God Himself.
Thank You and praise You for the transforming power of Jesus.
Through Him our lives can be alive and everlasting.
We can change.
We can grow.
We have everything we need in Jesus.
We can live in the Hope that only Jesus gives.
He is the Lamb of God!

In the same way, count yourselves dead to sin but alive to God in Christ Jesus. (Rom. 6:11)

Enjoy His presence: still yourself, listen, write

December 5

Full Coverage

Lord Jesus, You paid the full price for our sins.
Words cannot express our gratitude for Your gracious sacrifice
for us.
No sin is too big for Your Blood to cover.
Your Blood saves us.
Your Power raises us and enables us to overcome.
Thank You for the cross that brings freedom and forgiveness.
We have full coverage, granting eternal life when...
we confess our sins,
agree to turn from our sins,
accept You as Savior,
and choose to follow You all the days of our lives.
Thank You, Jesus, that Your Word covers us with the truth.
You forgive and forget.
Your Hand protects.
Your Power brings freedom.
We can rest in the assurance that we have full coverage in
Jesus.

*"Blessed are they whose transgressions are forgiven,
whose sins are covered. Blessed is the man whose sin the
Lord will never count against him."* (Rom. 4:7-8)

Enjoy His presence: still yourself, listen, write

Hallelujah! Amen. It is Done.

December 6

Practice

Mighty God, You are Above All.
Your grace is always present.
You are...
Strong,
Steady,
and Our Balance.
Father, when we stumble and fall, help us to remember that You're the One who picks us back up again.
Motivate us to seek you daily.
The daily practice of prayer and Bible study makes strong Christians.
Practicing prayer and studying Your Word strengthens our faith and brings balance in our lives.
We choose to stand strong for Jesus.
Help us to put into practice what He has shown us and what we know to be true.
Jesus is the Prince of Peace.

Whatever you have learned or received or heard from me, or seen in me---put it into practice. And the God of peace will be with you. (Phil. 4:9)

Enjoy His presence: still yourself, listen, write

December 7

Come and Trust...I AM in Your Corner

Thank You, Father, for providing the Way back to You.
Help people to place their faith in Jesus and what He did for them on the cross.
We can trust that His Blood saves lives.
His Blood washes away our sins.
Help us to trust Him and what He's done for us, and not what we can do or what we've done.
Holy Spirit, enlighten minds that salvation comes through Jesus alone, and not by our efforts or good works.
It is by God's grace that we have new life.
We can trust His Word.
Send Your Spirit to guide us into the truth and clear up doubts.
Jesus is the Answer.

"Come now, let us reason together," says the LORD. "Though your sins are like scarlet, they shall be as white as snow; though they are red as crimson, they shall be like wool." (Isaiah 1:18)

Enjoy His presence: still yourself, listen, write

Hallelujah! Amen. It is Done.

December 8

The Bridegroom

Lord Jesus, You're coming some day for all believers.
We are looking forward to seeing our Bridegroom!
Prepare all hearts to respond to Jesus.
Help people not to put off accepting Jesus as their Savior and Lord.
Each one of us individually makes the decision where we will spend eternity.
No one else can make that decision for us.
Holy Spirit, may people not delay.
These are days of grace.
This day may be someone's last day to accept Your Gift of eternal life.
Hold back the evil one from whispering, "Wait."
For today is the day of salvation.
The Bridegroom will come!

"At midnight the cry rang out: 'Here's the bridegroom! Come out to meet him!' " (Matt. 25:6)

Enjoy His presence: still yourself, listen, write

December 9

Finding You

Father, You want us to know You.

You constantly are pursuing us and giving us opportunities to know You more.

You want us to come to You the way we are.

No matter where we've been or what we've done, You are willing to forgive and forget.

You never dig up old hurts.

Help us, Lord, to forgive and forget old hurts from people in our past.

Enable us to drop those things that keep us from experiencing Your peace.

May we wholeheartedly look to Jesus for our comfort and peace.

We can find what we need in Jesus.

He is near to the brokenhearted.

Thank You, Father, that You are so willing to respond to our call for help.

You will seek me and find me when you seek me with all your heart. (Jer. 29:13)

Enjoy His presence: still yourself, listen, write

Hallelujah! Amen. It is Done.

December 10

No Drifters

All praise to You, Father, for giving us the Wonderful Gift of grace received only through Jesus Christ.

Jesus is Your Precious Gift to us.

He is Your plan for our salvation.

Help us to freely receive Your Gift of Grace and then live our lives in an attitude of thanksgiving.

May we be reminded that Your Gift of eternal life is not earned or given because of some special ability we have.

Protect us from any lie that would mislead us to think that our good works gets us to heaven.

May we never drift away from being grateful for Jesus' death on the cross.

Father, help us to be ever mindful of Your grace.

Let us bow to You and say...

thank You,

thank You,

for giving us Your Gift of Jesus.

For it is by grace you have been saved, through faith --- and this not from yourselves, it is the gift of God --- not by works, so that no one can boast. (Eph. 2:8-9)

Enjoy His presence: still yourself, listen, write

December 11

A Promise to Fight

You, O God, are a Mighty Warrior.
You come to the defense of Your servants.
You fight for us.
Your Hand is Strong.
You are Faithful and Your Greatness is beyond words.
Your Word reminds us often not to be scared because You go before us.
Thank You, Father, for Your great promise to protect and shield us.
You are our Covering.
You have us surrounded.
Help us, Father, to rest in the shadow of Jesus.
For without Him we have nothing but empty promises.
Help us to take hold of Jesus' Hand.
When He says He will fight for us...He will fight for us!

"Do not be afraid of them; the LORD your God himself will fight for you." (Deu. 3:22)

Enjoy His presence: still yourself, listen, write

Hallelujah! Amen. It is Done.

December 12

Bring Us Together

Father, You created each one of us, and You don't make mistakes.

Each one of us was created to be a reflection of You.

Help us to treat people who are different the way Jesus would treat them.

Forgive us when we think we are better or more special in Your eyes.

You died for each one of us.

Your Love shows no favoritism.

Bring us together, no matter how different we look or act.

Help us to respond to Your call to love one another.

We choose to encourage one another, and look at each other through eyes of grace.

And let us consider how we may spur one another on toward love and good deeds. Let us not give up meeting together, as some are in the habit of doing, but let us encourage one another---and all the more as you see the Day approaching. (Heb. 10:24-25)

Enjoy His presence: still yourself, listen, write

December 13

Beautiful Feet

Gracious Father, thank You for giving us Jesus, our Beautiful Savior.
He provides for our greatest need…to be cleansed from sin.
He is Your One and Only Son and whoever believes in Him will live forever.
This is the truth, because You said so.
You cannot lie.
Hold back any twist of the truth about Jesus.
Stop people from discoloring the good news about Him.
You are Holy God.
We are sinners.
We need a Savior.
Jesus was the Perfect Sacrifice for our sins.
He died for us.
He rose from the dead.
He is alive!
He is Lord over all.
Thank You for the gospel of Jesus Christ.
That's good news!

As it is written, "How beautiful are the feet of those who bring good news!" (Rom. 10:15)

Enjoy His presence: still yourself, listen, write

Hallelujah! Amen. It is Done.

December 14

They Walk Blameless

Jesus, Gracious and Merciful God, thank You for Your great Love.
Thank You for encouraging us to stay focused on You, and keep walking with You.
Teach us to...
see,
hear,
and know Your will and way.
Enable us to live our lives according to God's Word.
We humbly say, "Lead on."
We desire to follow You.
We choose to love You wholeheartedly.
It is by Your grace and mercy, that true believers walk blamelessly, devoted to You.

Not that I have already obtained all this, or have already been made perfect, but I press on to take hold of that for which Christ Jesus took hold of me. (Phil. 3:12)

Enjoy His presence: still yourself, listen, write

December 15

Friction

We praise You, Father, for being our Comforter.
You know the friction we can feel in our...
families,
jobs,
communities,
and in the world.
We need Your intervention.
Touch relationships with Your...
compassion,
patience,
and mercy.
Bring Your soothing touch in our lives.
Help us to be channels of Your grace to one another, and not a source of irritation.
Help us to look at others, like You look at us...through eyes of grace.

Yet the LORD longs to be gracious to you; he rises to show you compassion. (Isaiah 30:18)

Enjoy His presence: still yourself, listen, write

Hallelujah! Amen. It is Done.

December 16

Sleep

We praise You, Jesus, for being the Prince of Peace.
You are the Pain Reliever.
You bring calmness.
We ask that You guard our sleep.
Give us a good night's rest.
Help all those that are having trouble sleeping to feel Your peaceful presence.
Most of all, may they rest in the assurance of having a personal relationship with You....the Prince of Peace.

I will lie down and sleep in peace, for you alone, O LORD, make me dwell in safety. (Psalm 4:8)

Enjoy His presence: still yourself, listen, write

December 17

Breath of God

Father, Your Son Jesus, is the Prince of Peace.
You give true Peace.
There are many things that try to steal our peace...
health issues,
pressures at work,
money,
raising children,
and the condition of the world.
But, Your Peace is powerful and real.
It's not like anything the world offers.
Your Peace is a Gift.
Your Peace is empowering.
You give us the strength to keep going no matter where You send us.
When we study Your Word and pray it's like taking a big breath of God.
The peace Jesus gives is like oxygen, which gives life and rest to our weary souls.
Holy Spirit, help us daily to breathe in Your Peace.

Again Jesus said, "Peace be with you! As the Father has sent me, I am sending you." And with that he breathed on them and said, "Receive the Holy Spirit." (John 20:21-22)

Enjoy His presence: still yourself, listen, write

Hallelujah! Amen. It is Done.

December 18

Belt of Truth

O God, thank You for securely attaching the belt of truth around our waist.
Thank You for Your Mighty power.
May we learn to trust You more and more each day.
Instill in us the discipline to spend time with You in prayer.
Increase in us a hunger to know the truth of Your Word.
Help us to stand firm and not give into any type of lie.
Guard us from the schemes of the devil.
Praise to You, Father God!
The devil is no match for You.
For You are above all, and You alone are God.

Stand firm then, with the belt of truth buckled around your waist, with the breastplate of righteousness in place. (Eph. 6:14)

Enjoy His presence: still yourself, listen, write

December 19

The Highest

Father God, You are the Highest!
You are Number One.
You are First and Last.
You are Almighty.
You are the Winner.
This battle is Yours.
Thank You for fighting for us.
You are our Advocate and Defender.
You are in control even when things are falling apart.
You are able to hold us together.
You are the Armor that protects us.
Nothing can snatch Your children out of Your Hand.
You have a hold on us.
Thank You for Your Spirit that enables us to stand strong.
You are...Most High!

He who dwells in the shelter of the Most High will rest in the shadow of the Almighty. (Psalm 91:1)

Enjoy His presence: still yourself, listen, write

Hallelujah! Amen. It is Done.

December 20

Trying Too Hard

Jesus, Our Lord, thank You for taking care of every part of our lives.
Help us to trust You more.
Deepen our relationship with You.
Remind us that we walk every minute in Your strength.
Help us to stop trying so hard.
It's so easy to try to muscle through life on our own strength.
May we rest in Your strength and Your will for us.
Help Your children walk through their lives step by step, day by day, and sometimes moment by moment.
Keep us forever mindful of Your loving presence along the way.

My salvation and my honor depend on God; he is my mighty rock, my refuge. (Psalm 62:7)

Enjoy His presence: still yourself, listen, write

December 21

Resting in You

Lord God, You are the Protector.
You take care of us at all times.
Even when we're not aware of danger, Your Power surrounds us.
Help us to rest in the assurance that no matter what, You are in control.
You are Sovereign and nothing can shake You.
You always keep Your promises.
You said You're coming back.
We look forward to the day when every knee will bow to You, because You are Lord God Almighty.
As we wait for You, empower us to...
be ready,
watch,
and be found resting in You.

"Be still, and know that I am God; I will be exalted among the nations, I will be exalted in the earth." The LORD Almighty is with us; the God of Jacob is our fortress. (Psalm 46:10-11)

Enjoy His presence: still yourself, listen, write

Hallelujah! Amen. It is Done.

December 22

Wolves

All Powerful and All Knowing God, deliver us from deceit and false teachings.
Jesus is the Truth.
Demolish any strong-hold in our lives.
Help us to recognize any twisted, deceitful tactics of the evil one.
Protect us, Lord Jesus, from people who appear to know You, but they really don't know You.
We ask for wisdom and discernment, so we may recognize and flee from the lies of the enemy.
Sovereign Lord, You are the Winner and the evil one is the loser.
Thank You for the victory that is ours...through Jesus Christ.

Watch out for false prophets. They come to you in sheep's clothing, but inwardly they are ferocious wolves. (Matt. 7:15)

Enjoy His presence: still yourself, listen, write

December 23

Hands of Healing

Jesus, Your Hands are Hands of Healing.
You bring...
peace,
wholeness,
relief,
and forgiveness.
Almighty God, You are more than able to remove the dirt and ugliness in our lives and bring blessings.
Help us to give the dirty part of our lives to You.
Help us to empty our hands and place everything in Jesus' Healing Hands.
His Hands are always extended with an on-going invitation to accept His Gift of Grace.
Remind us daily that You have a special place prepared for believers, where there is no more suffering or tears.
Thank You, Father, that we are ultimately healed through Jesus Christ.

He lifted me out of the slimy pit, out of the mud and mire; he set my feet on a rock and gave me a firm place to stand. He put a new song in my mouth, a hymn of praise to our God. (Psalm 40:2-3)

Enjoy His presence: still yourself, listen, write

Hallelujah! Amen. It is Done.

December 24

Offering

Thank You, Jesus, for coming into this world as the Perfect Offering.
You are the Lamb of God.
Thank You, Jesus, that You obeyed our Father's will.
You died for the forgiveness of our sins.
Create in us a spirit of forgiveness, like Jesus.
Help us to have a sacrificial love for others, like Jesus.
Fill us with Your enabling power, to become more like Him.
With faith in Jesus, and covered by His Blood…we offer ourselves to You.

Be imitators of God, therefore, as dearly loved children and live a life of love, just as Christ loved us and gave himself up for us as a fragrant offering and sacrifice to God. (Eph. 5:1-2)

Enjoy His presence: still yourself, listen, write

The Gift of Jesus

Father, You are the Gift-Giver.
Jesus, the Savior of the world was born.
Thank You for the Gift of Jesus.
Your Way is Gracious and Wondrous.
Your Word says that when we...
repent of our sins,
believe in Jesus,
and follow the Lord...His Gift of eternal life is ours.
Father, You are...
Mighty,
Wonderful,
Everlasting,
and the Winner.
Hold back evil and protect us from lies that want to twist the truth.
Open minds and hearts to accept Jesus as Savior and Lord.
Thank You for these days of grace.

For to us a child is born, to us a son is given, and the government will be on his shoulders. And he will be called Wonderful Counselor, Mighty God, Everlasting Father, Prince of Peace. (Isaiah 9:6)

Enjoy His presence: still yourself, listen, write

Hallelujah! Amen. It is Done.

December 26

Blend Us

Loving Father, thank You for making each one of us unique.
Take away anything that makes another person feel less.
We ask that You knock down "one-up" attitudes.
Do away with an unbalanced competitive spirit.
May our diversity be our strength.
Blend us together in Your Spirit.
Smooth us into a mixture of caring and supportive servants.
Father, blend Jesus into our…
families,
churches,
communities,
and the world.

"I in them and you in me. May they be brought to complete unity to let the world know that you sent me and have loved them even as you have loved me." (John 17:23)

Enjoy His presence: still yourself, listen, write

December 27

Reality

Father, Your Word is true.
You don't tell lies.
You don't exaggerate or make up stuff.
What You say is real.
Oftentimes we like to live in a fairy tale world.
We can easily find ourselves pretending and choosing not to look at ourselves the way we really are.
Help us to stop pretending that we...
have all the answers,
can do things in our own strength,
and can save ourselves.
The reality is that, no matter how good we act, it's not good enough before a Holy God.
Our greatest need is to be cleansed from sin.
The truth is...we all need Jesus.
His Blood alone saves us.
May we come to the reality of what Jesus did for us on the Cross.
He is the Redeemer.

In him we have redemption through his blood, the forgiveness of sins, in accordance with the riches of God's grace. (Eph. 1:7)

Enjoy His presence: still yourself, listen, write

Hallelujah! Amen. It is Done.

December 28

Battling Prayer

Father, Your sustaining Power is beyond our capabilities.
Your Power brings…
strength,
confidence,
deliverance,
and protection.
You are, our Defender.
Thank You, Jesus, that You are always battling for us in prayer.
Surrendering to Jesus as Savior and Lord grants us the holy privilege of praying with You.
We join Your lead in prayer.
We want what You want.
Help us to listen.
Help us to trust.
Teach us more about prayer.
Thank You for the joy that comes when we give our battles to You in prayer.

And pray in the Spirit on all occasions with all kinds of prayers and requests. With this in mind, be alert and always keep on praying for all the saints. (Eph. 6:18)

Enjoy His presence: still yourself, listen, write

December 29

Your Boundaries

Jesus, You always knew when to be still and when to speak.
Make us more like You.
Guard our tongues so we say things that sound like what You would say.
Lord, help us to have the discipline it takes to stay within the boundaries You have set before us as Christians.
You have given us boundaries that separate...
communication from gossip,
encouragement from criticism,
and the truth from the twist of the truth.
Help us to respond to Your call to move and grow.
Move our hearts.
May we grow in Christian godliness as we learn when to speak and when to be still.
We praise You for Your Mercy and Grace!

Avoid godless chatter, because those who indulge in it will become more and more ungodly. (2 Tim. 2:16)

Enjoy His presence: still yourself, listen, write

Hallelujah! Amen. It is Done.

December 30

Our Deliverer

In Your Name, Jesus, deliver us from fear and confusion.
With You there is nothing to be afraid of.
Help us to choose to praise You.
You are...
the Strongest,
our Helper,
our Protector,
and our Guide forever.
May we respond to Your call to grow deeper with You.
Help us to come and experience...
the fire of Your love,
the fire of Your knowledge,
the fire of Your power,
and the fire of Your protection.
May we come to You with the assurance in our minds and hearts
that we stand in the presence of a loving God who delivers!

***So do not fear, for I am with you; do not be dismayed, for
I am your God. I will strengthen you and help you; I will
uphold you with my righteous right hand.*** (Isaiah 41:10)

Enjoy His presence: still yourself, listen, write

December 31

In Joy

Father, You love to delight us and surprise us.
You are fun.
You love it when we laugh.
You originally created this earth as a means of enjoyment for us.
And You are preparing a place right now for us to enjoy forevermore with You.
You love being with us.
And we love being with You.
There is great joy in Your presence.
Help us to relax and remember Your promise that no matter what we're going through, or where we are, You are with us.
What joy it is to know the truth.
You will never leave us.
You are holding us and pulling us through.
Help us to hear You whisper to our hearts, "It's going to be okay."
Help us, Lord, to...
stay centered on You,
spend time in Your Word,
trust You,
and submit everything to You.
Help us to live in joy, no matter what direction You take us.
To Jesus be the glory!

"And surely I am with you always, to the very end of the age." (Matt. 28:20)

Enjoy His presence: still yourself, listen, write

Hallelujah! Amen. It is Done.